RICE IN THE STORM

Faith in Struggle in the Philippines

edited by Rebecca C. Asedillo and B. David Williams

FRIENDSHIP PRESS ● NEW YORK

Library of Congress Cataloging-in-Publication Data

Rice in the storm: faith in struggle in the Philippines / editors.
Rebecca C. Asedillo and B. David Williams.
  p.   cm.
  ISBN 0-377-00192-9 : $6.95
  1. Christianity—Philippines. 2. Church and social problems—
Philippines. I. Asedillo, Rebecca C., 1950- . II. Williams, B.
David.
  BR1260.R53 1989
  275.99′082—dc19

                                   88-38787
                                        CIP

Unless otherwise stated, all Bible quotations in this book
are from the Revised Standard Version, copyright 1946 and
1952 by the Division of Christian Education of the National
Council of the Churches of Christ in the United States of
America. Quotations have in certain instances been edited
for inclusive language according to that organization's
guidelines.

Map drawn by Sean Grandits

ISBN 0-377-00192-9

Editorial Offices: 475 Riverside Drive, Room 772, New York,
NY 10115
Distribution Offices: P.O. Box 37844, Cincinnati, OH 45222
Copyright © 1989 Friendship Press, Inc.
Printed in the United States of America

A WORD OF THANKS

In addition to our principal contributors, the editors wish to express appreciation for valued support to the following: Vicky Apuan; Byron W. Clark; Sandy Galzazin, M.M.; Gary N. Gamer; Mary Grenough, M.M.; Edwin M. Luidens; Mario R. Mapanao; Carlos R. Ocampo; T. Valentino Sitoy, Jr.; and Lloyd G. Van Vactor.

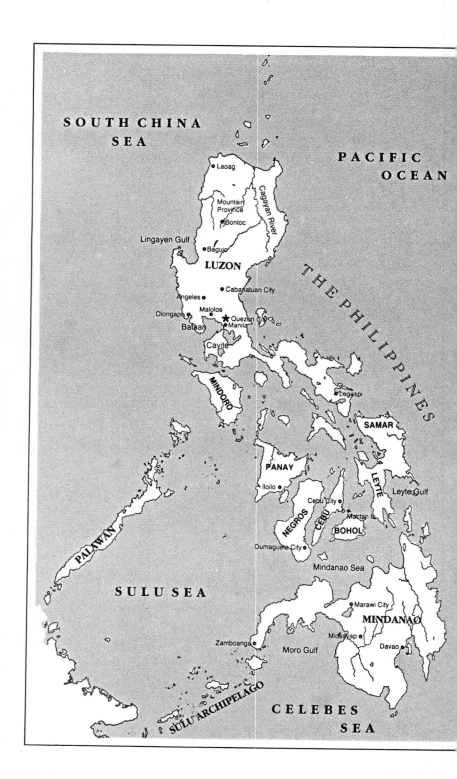

SOUTH CHINA
SEA

PACIFIC
OCEAN

• Laoag

Mountain
Province
• Bontoc

Lingayen Gulf

• Baguio

Cagayan River

THE PHILIPPINES

LUZON

• Cabanatuan City

Angeles •

Malolos
Olongapo •   ★ Quezon City
Bataan   • Manila

Cavite

MINDORO

• Legaspi

SAMAR

PANAY

LEYTE

Iloilo •

Leyte Gulf

Cebu City •

Mactan Is.

NEGROS

CEBU

BOHOL

PALAWAN

Dumaguete City •

Mindanao Sea

SULU SEA

• Marawi City

MINDANAO

Midsayap •

Davao •

Zamboanga •

Moro Gulf

SULU ARCHIPELAGO

CELEBES
SEA

CONTENTS

FOREWORD

We are a struggling people. From the advent of Western colonial rule as established by Spain and the neo-colonial rule of the United States of America to the toppling of a dictatorship and the process of rebuilding a broken nation, we Filipinos have struggled to establish God's rule of dignity, justice, freedom, equality and peace in our bleeding land.

This struggle has been chronicled in our rich literary heritage—in ballads, poetry, stories, songs and liturgies. It is enshrined in the lives of people from all parts of our society who have unselfishly laid down their lives for our motherland. It is hallowed by the blood of our martyrs, who have come, and continue to come from the ranks of peasants, laborers, fisherfolk, students, professionals and nationalist businesspersons, and from the church.

Yes, the church has given the lives of its clergy and lay workers to the quest for freedom and peace. Churchpersons like Gregorio Aglipay, Hermano Pule, Zacarias Agatep and countless unnamed others have ushered in a new dimension of mission for the church. They have paved the way for a new ecumenism that transcends old definitions. It is an ecumenism that "has come out of the Church's ministry in identity and solidarity with the people's struggle for justice, peace, and freedom," and whose main objective is the "restoration of the individual to full humanhood and the transformation of society to usher in the Kingdom of God." (From the 1986 Polity Statement on Ecumenical Relations of the United Church of Christ in the Philippines.)

These objectives of restoration and transformation are far from accomplished. While the Filipino people have unshackled the chains of repression and tyranny of the recent dictatorship, we find that we are once more being drawn into the vortex of crisis. In a brief span of time, the bright new sun that dawned on our land is being replaced by a cloud of gloom. The "democratic space" brought about by the new government proved to be the calm before the storm. An objective look at our situation will show that the impoverished sectors of our society—the peasants, laborers and urban poor—groan under the burden of increasing poverty. Their cries of anguish and protest have been met with repressive measures, or worse, with the thud of a bullet. Traditional politics have returned. The old political system of personalities, patronage and power-brokering has been revived. Polarization has increased. Pluralism, a hallmark of any democracy, is being relegated to the sidelines by the clever machinations of those who see things in black and white, never with the shades of gray that real life presents. Human rights are still being violated and perpetuated by armed groups of all sorts.

One reason why we in the Philippines consider this study so important is that the United States government continues repeatedly to interfere in our national affairs and processes in order to safeguard its economic and military interests. The U.S. has given substantial amounts of military aid to help quell the rising sentiments of our people for national sovereignty. It has used the media to portray freedom-loving Filipinos as godless ideologues who are out to grab power (as if the ideology of capitalism were godly!). More alarming, the sacred Scriptures are being used by certain evangelists to reduce our arguments for change into the terms of an other-worldly battle between good and evil.

Our long years of struggle have proven to us that as long as foreigners control us, whether directly or indirectly, we will continue to suffer dependency and injustice. We have, however, come to realize that many individual Americans (as distinguished from their government), particularly our sisters and brothers in the faith, are our friends and companions in our struggle. The fact that the American people once cast off the bonds of British colonialism has taught us the valuable lesson that freedom is never given; it is something that must be taken.

We are glad that the Program Committee on Education for Mission of the National Council of the Churches of Christ in the USA has chosen the Philippines as the geographic focus of its mission study for 1989-90. This is most timely, considering the current re-negotiations of the U.S.-Philippines Military Bases Agreement, the principal locus of American presence and intervention in Philippine affairs. It is our hope that this study will help American churchpeople and others to better understand the truth of what is happening in our troubled land. Too often, what is portrayed about our situation in the mass media is badly distorted.

I pray that this study will draw our churches and our peoples into closer companionship on our separate, yet common pilgrimage of faith. For us this is a pilgrimage of Life in a world beset by Death. We yearn for a world in which people regard one another with respect; a world of peace in which all peoples and nations are given the chance to carve out their own unique identities and destinies in a world united in justice and right relationships under God's rule.

The God of life, freedom, justice and peace be with us all!

Bishop Erme R. Camba
General Secretary
United Church of Christ in the Philippines
March, 1988

INTRODUCTION

How our hopes soared when in February 1986, millions of Filipinos stood together in the streets, many of them in front of tanks and machine guns, peacefully but with incredible people's power, to confirm the end of the Marcos dictatorship! People who had never before in their lives joined a demonstration went out this time, with conviction. Stories and now books abound which attempt to share what happened, to convey the sense of new possibilities, the excitement of the new "feeling."

The whole world took notice, and dictators literally trembled as they watched not only the events in the Philippines but the fall of Duvalier in Haiti just days earlier and the masses of people protesting in the streets of Seoul. For several days, many of us in North America remained glued to our television sets.

How many people told us that they had "goose pimples," or said, "I'm so proud to be a Filipino!" Vivid images of courage and caring remain.

But while something extraordinary did indeed happen during those days, we now face the sobering reality that what we were witnessing was basically a transfer of power, not the social and political transformation that was so desperately needed. The struggles of the Filipino people for fundamental change continue.

Of particular note for us is that religious faith, particularly Christian faith, also continues to be in struggle in the Philippines. But then, true Christian faith is always at risk against forces within the life of the church that would limit people's faith response to one of narrow, private spirituality. It is always

struggling for deeper meaning and purpose in the face
of simplistic and often mean-spirited answers;
struggling to stand in greater solidarity with the poor,
particularly the poor who have organized themselves;
struggling against every violation of life, whether
dramatic or subtle.

The chapters in this book represent voices in the
Philippines that are raising critical, sometimes divisive
issues related to Christian mission today. Critically yet
responsibly, these voices seek a deeper understanding
of what it will mean for Christians to be in mission
in the Philippines in the 1990s. What does faithfulness
mean in the Philippines today? How must the Gospel
of Jesus Christ be defined, articulated, lived out, in the
words of Bishop LaVerne Mercado, "at the bleeding
points of history"?

This study is also an affirmation and a celebration
of the life of the Filipino people. It recognizes their
uniqueness as a people, their exceptional gifts and their
enduring problems. Here is a beautiful, rich land, a
gifted and energetic people—yet unbending poverty
crushes the lives of the overwhelming majority. If we
take Christian mission seriously, we must be willing,
as North American churchpeople, to face the hard
questions Filipinos are raising.

We are delighted to include in this book chapters
by Roman Catholic leaders, a most appropriate
recognition of the critical role the Roman Catholic
Church has played in the Philippines, both historically
and at present.

A substantial portion of the material in this book
has been prepared by women. This is one way, however
modest, to reflect the central role, present and past,
played by Filipino women in the life of the church
and in the struggles of the poor.

We do not pretend that the point of view presented
in this book is the only point of view, nor even the
predominant point of view found among church-people
in the Philippines. We think, however, that it is a biblical
point of view, one not paid sufficient attention in North
America, and one that urgently challenges us at this

moment in history. It is presented to stimulate North
American Christians to deeper searching and to call
us all to reflection and dialogue.

We recognize that in both North America and in the
Philippines there are some who are critical of the
church, perhaps justifiably so, and some who have
given up on the church. We would point out to North
Americans that no institution has a deeper engagement
with the reality of Philippine life at the grassroots level
than does the church. Many Filipino Christians and
some foreign missionaries, as a direct expression of their
faith, have shared deeply in the suffering of those who
have taken determined stands for justice.

Filipino Christians have much to teach us out of their
experience of struggle in an incredibly dynamic,
polarized context. They are dealing with painful but
inescapable choices. The Philippines is a deeply divided
society, and the churches reflect that. Friendships,
family loyalties and even marriages are being tested,
sharply. What do Christians do in such difficult and
violent situations?

We hope that some of the articles that follow will
reflect the nature of the "spirituality of struggle" that
is emerging in the Philippines, a spiritual focus not
unlike that emerging in other parts of the Third World.
As North Americans encounter this increasingly
important spiritual tradition, the question inevitably
arises: What, indeed, is the form *our own* spirituality
should take? What is *our own* distinctive "people's
theology?" We can expect that the North American
answer may have both positive and negative
dimensions.

Most of the selections in this book will be a distinct
challenge for North American readers, particularly for
U.S. Christians as they are reminded of their country's
past and continuing impact on the life and land of the
Filipino people. Yet some readers may still wonder:
"What do these questions, most of them so political,
have to do with Christian mission?" We can only
respond that when decisions made in the chambers
of the Pentagon or in the back rooms of the U.S. National

Security Council or in the boardrooms of transnational corporations have greater effect upon the everyday well-being of Filipinos than do the efforts of Christian missionaries, we had better take a hard look at them! Seen in overview, the current Philippine crisis reflects the following historic elements, which continue to converge:

People's movements: Since Spanish times, Filipinos have organized people's movements in attempts to confront injustices and to fulfil their aspirations for economic and political self-determination. In the first years after U.S. occupation began in 1898, hundreds of thousands of Filipinos were killed by American soldiers who brutally put down a popular independence struggle. For centuries, Filipino priests and church laypeople have been among those struggling for self-determination. This has been felt strongly in Protestant as well as Roman Catholic church life. Up to now, Filipinos' national aspirations remain largely unfulfilled.

Foreign control of the economy: An export economy based on the exploitative sharecropping system was developed under Spanish colonial rule. When the U.S. assumed the dominant role the pattern continued, and in some ways the situation became worse as Philippine dependency extended to more and more areas of the economy. While new actors such as Japan later entered the scene, the system established in colonial times remains intact. Rural poverty and agrarian problems, characteristic of the Spanish period, became even more serious under American rule. After World War II, expanding U.S. corporate agribusiness added heavily to the problems.

The power of elite groups: Privileged groups of Filipinos that had formed during the Spanish period easily shifted their loyalties to the U.S. colonial adminis-tration. They continue to weigh heavily in the political process today, and have been greatly responsible for obstructing fundamental reform. They have also been a major force in the creation of right-wing armed groups and have encouraged militarization in general.

The church: From Spanish times, the church has been an integral part of the life of the Philippines in a most intimate, complex way that is full of contradictions. The church was the conveyer of the gospel, yet a primary instrument in the colonization process. It has been an established institution resisting change, yet a vehicle for the imposition of Western culture. It has promoted an ideal of charity that has often obscured the root causes of problems, yet it has proclaimed truth, justice and liberation. The identification of the Spanish friars with Spanish political power and American missionaries with U.S. interests is a reality with which Filipino and American Christians must struggle. Today the church is challenged to work for transformation in its own life and to take a redemptive role in the current crisis. Unfortunately, some of its most dedicated leaders, both clergy and lay, are deceptively labelled "communist" for their identification with the people. The list of martyrs is too long, and is growing.

U.S. interests: For nearly a century, American geopolitical and economic interests have dominated Philippine political development. Today, the economic dimension, while overbearing at times, is largely overshadowed by perceived "national security" (military-strategic) interests. In recent years, intervention has become more direct and overt. In a word, the U.S. continues on a collision course with the democratic aspirations of the Filipino people.

In many ways the current military and political conflict in the Philippines—especially in relation to the policy objectives of the U.S. and perhaps even in relation to the church—is reminiscent of the period of the

Philippine-American war at the turn of the century. We hope that the references to that time will be illuminating and will lead many of those who take part in this study to take action for justice.

While only Filipinos themselves can bring authentic democracy to their land, U.S. policy and action will strongly affect their efforts to reach this elusive goal. Most Filipinos would agree that the unique U.S.-Philippine relationship, strangely intimate due to historical, religious and immigration factors, should not be broken. But it cries out for renewal. The church must be a part of that renewal.

Rebecca C. Asedillo and B. David Williams

Dawn in Tacaloban City on the island of Leyte. While most people think of the Philippines as a Roman Catholic country, it is a national community of great religious diversity. Note the Buddhist temple and the indigenous Iglesia ni Kristo in the background of this photograph

THE FILIPINO PEOPLE

Mary John Mananzan, O.S.B.

The Filipino people are mainly of Malay-Polynesian stock enriched by Chinese and Spanish blood. The archipelago they call home is made up of 7,100 islands with a total land area of about 115,600 square miles. These islands are distributed from north to south along three main island groups: Luzon, the Visayas and Mindanao.

Because this archipelago is located at the northeastern end of a historic route from Arabia and India to Southeast Asia and is blocked by the Malaysian peninsula, the Islamic and Hindu cultural influences that permeate present-day Southeast Asia are not dominant features of Filipino culture. Islam was just gaining a foothold in southern Mindanao when Spanish colonization interrupted its growth. Today, an overwhelming majority of Filipinos (92 percent) profess themselves Christian, 85 percent Catholic and 6 percent Protestant. Slightly more than 5 percent are Muslims. The 57 million Filipinos communicate with one another in eight language groups with a total of about 87 dialects; the upper and middle classes are predominantly English-speaking.

A history of struggle

The history of the Filipino people is one of struggle.

Mary John Mananzan, a Benedictine sister, is dean of Santa Scholastic University in Manila. She has a Ph.D. in theology and has written extensively in the area of Philippine church history. She has studied in Germany and at the Gregorian University in Rome.

It is an ancient, unfinished struggle against various forms of oppression and tyranny from the conquest and colonization of the Spaniards in the sixteenth century through the American annexation in 1898, the Japanese occupation of World War II, the martial law years under Ferdinand Marcos, and now under a pervasive and deeply rooted neo-colonialism.*

Pre-colonial Philippines

Arriving in 1521, the Spanish *conquistadores* found the archipelago (which was eventually to be named after Philip II of Spain) to be a land of scattered communities with no central government or consciousness as a nation. Each community was ruled by a *datu*. The settlement was called a *barangay*, after the ocean-going boats that had brought Malaysian migrants to the islands.

Pre-colonial Filipino society had three social classes: nobles, freemen and dependents. The nobility enjoyed much power, and bore such titles as *gat* or *lakan*. The *alipins*, or dependents, occupied the lowest rank either by inheritance, captivity, purchase or failure to pay debts. However, there were no rigid lines between the classes, and an *alipin* could become a *maharlika*, or freeman, either by paying his debt or performing a heroic deed.

A remarkable feature of pre-colonial Philippine society was the position of women, which the Filipino historian Agoncillo describes in the following manner:

> In such a society the position of women was unique; customary laws gave them the right to be the equal of men in certain respects; for they could own and inherit property, engage in trade and industry, and succeed to the leadership of the

---

* One rather specific definition of neo-colonialism: "An alliance between the leading class or classes of two independent nations which facilitates their ability to maintain a dominant position over the rest of the population of the weaker of the two nations." (Shalom, Stephen R., *The U.S. and the Philippines: A Study of Neocolonialism.* Philadelphia: Institute for the Study of Human Issues, 1981.)

community in the absence of a male heir. Significantly, the women also enjoyed the exclusive right to give names to their children.[1]

By and large, the people had a subsistence economy that was based mainly in agriculture. Trade subsequently developed in such areas as poultry, fishing, stockraising, mining, lumbering, weaving and shipbuilding. In years when enough surplus was produced, domestic trade, primarily by means of barter, was carried on among the numerous islands and communities. A brisk trade also developed with such neighboring countries as China, Japan, Siam, Borneo, Sumatra and Java.

The people had a basically Malayan culture. Written languages were used not only for communication but also for literary expression to celebrate the significant moments of life. Folk epics were handed down from one generation to another.[*]

Political and economic relationships were informal and government was based on kinship rather than on law. The Muslim islands were an exception to this, having a more sophisticated form of administration under a *rajah* or *sultan*, along with a relatively more advanced culture and more developed political and religious organizations.

Most people in the ancient cultures believed in a supreme deity called "Bathala," whose name, interestingly enough, was made up of the first syllable of the word for woman (*ba*bae) and the first syllable of the word for man (*la*lake) connected by a syllable that meant "spirit" or "light." Thus the name of the fundamental deity was non-sexist, and could mean "the union of woman and man in light or spirit."[2]

Aside from Bathala there were lesser spirits (now commonly called *anitos*) in the native pantheon. These were the spirits of the ancestors that inhabited the trees, the hills, and nature in general. Sacrifices were offered at important occasions of life: at birth, weddings,

---

[*] See the Maguindanao folk epic in the *The Sari-Sari Store: A Philippine Scrapbook (Friendship Press, 1989).*

harvest times, at death. There was also a belief in life
after death.

The lack of political unity and national consciousness,
as well as the lack of a complex religious system facilitated the easy conquest of the Philippines by Spain.

The Philippines under Spain

At dawn on October 19, 1469, Ferdinand, King of Sicily,
and Isabella, heiress to the throne of Castille, were
quietly married at a private residence in Valladolid,
Spain. At this moment no one, not even the bride and
groom, fully realized the monumental significance of
this secretly arranged event, not only for the history
of Spain but for that of the entire world. For it was
during the reign of this couple, so-called *los Reyes
Catolicos*, that two major tasks would be accomplished:
the reconquest of the Spanish kingdom from the
Muslims and the subsequent discovery and unifica-
tion of the New World.

It was in the context of this grandiose project that
the voyage was launched which brought the Western
world to the Philippines. Magellan arrived in the islands
on March 17, 1521, but had no chance to colonize the
land because he was killed by the inhabitants of Cebu.
His surviving companions continued their voyage and
returned to Spain. The official colonization of the
Philippines began with Miguel Lopez de Legaspi, who
arrived forty-four years later, in February 1565.

The Spaniards set out to pacify and conquer the islands using the strategy of divide-and-rule. They
started with the Visayan islands and moved north towards Luzon. Spanish missionaries played a significant role in the conquest, introducing Christianity to
the islands as a part of colonization—a fact that would
identify the church with wealth and power in the minds
of the Filipino people. Indeed, the *patronato real* (literally,
royal patronage) given to the Spanish monarchs gave
them much power in ecclesiastical affairs.

Side by side with the Spanish soldiers and
sometimes preceding them, the missionaries

began the two-fold task of conquering the inhabitants, whom they would call *indios*, for Spain and for the Church. This collaboration of the cross and sword in the colonization of the Philippines would later become a problem in the minds of Filipino Christians because it shows very clearly the ideological function the Church played in the Spanish conquest of the Philippines. This is further underlined by the attempts of the Spanish theologians to justify the conquest and Spanish rule in the Philippines. Not finding any legal justification, they used the right of propagation of the faith and the right to protect the newly converted Christians for legitimation of the already accomplished acts of [conquest].[3]

The Spanish colonial administrators established a highly centralized government. A governor general was head, with broad executive, legislative and judicial powers. A system that apportioned parts of the colony among those who helped in its conquest was likewise introduced. This would eventually foment conflict because of abuses by the *encomenderos* (those who were given the land). The country was administered directly by the Viceroy of Mexico, with local governments patterned after the Mexican experience. The structure of the local government is described by Agoncillo:

The pre-colonial datus and rajahs and their descendants were chosen by the Spanish administrators to act as middlemen between the colonizers and the colonized. The town, consisting of several barrios or villages, was administered by the native *gobernadorcillos*... today the equivalent of town mayor, while the village was placed under the administration of the *cabeza de barangay*, whose duty was to collect tribute from the people of the village. There were other petty town officials who, together with the mayor and the village headman, constituted the native aristocracy.[4]

A judicial body called the *Royal Audiencia* was composed to investigate outgoing administrative officials or to carry out public hearings. The Spaniards were not noted for their economic success. In fact, agriculture and industry were neglected in favor of the "galleon trade." This was the name given to trade via Manila and Acapulco, which was the principal source of individual and official income. The result was the deterioration of the colony's economy. Only in the latter part of the eighteenth century, during the rule of the colonial administrators Bustamante and Basco, were economic reforms instituted to remedy this. In 1834 Manila was opened to world trade, which led to more development in agriculture, communication and transportation. But the fact of economic underdevelopment remained, a problem not unusual in former colonies of Spain.

Christianity was undoubtedly Spain's most significant legacy to the Philippines. The archipelago was divided into missionary areas and "distributed" to the first five missionary congregations (orders) to arrive in the Philippines: the Augustinians (1565), the Franciscans (1577), the Jesuits (1581), the Dominicans (1587) and the Augustinian Recoletos (1606).

Although the Filipino people received Christianity selectively and blended it with their existing beliefs and customs, there were great numbers of converts—a total of 250,000 in 1586 and 660,000 in 1591. In 1597, the administration of the church was formally launched with the establishment of the diocese of Manila. Catholic schools and seminaries were opened, and with this began the shaping of the Filipinos' culture according to "Christian" values and norms.

The parish priest, usually a friar, assumed a dominant role in the local community; eventually the friars became symbols of Spanish rule. However, people never really gave up their pre-colonial beliefs and practices, and these have remained to give Philippine Christianity its particular nuance and flavor (see page 24).

During the entire history of Spanish rule there were at least a hundred rebellions, beginning when Lapu-Lapu killed Magellan. Intermittent uprisings came about as a result of the levying of tribute, the practice of forced labor, the economic exploitation of farmers, discrimination and political oppression. There were revolts in the Pangasinan and Ilocos regions against discrimination and political oppression. In the Tagalog region there were revolts that challenged ecclesiastical landgrabbing, and in the Visayan region, revolts that showed messianic or millenarian characteristics. Most were quelled by the use of the divide-and-rule strategy. The historian Constantino points out the significance of these early revolts:

> The most fundamental aspect of Philippine history is the history of the struggle of its people for freedom and a better life. It was in the course of anti-colonial struggles against Spain that the native inhabitants of the archipelago gradually became conscious of their identity as one nation. But because colonial rule was established at an early stage of the people's social development and was maintained with but a short interregnum up to the twentieth century, the people's rebellions were for the most part negative responses to colonial oppression rather than positive movement for the attainment of national goals.[5]

He concludes, however: "Each successful uprising was a step in their political awakening. Each local revolt was a contribution to national consciousness."[6]

National consciousness would again be awakened in the latter part of the nineteenth century, especially in the Propaganda Movement led by Dr. Jose Rizal and other European-educated *ilustrados*. It reached a peak in the formation of the revolutionary movement called Katipunan, led by Andres Bonifacio, who started the Philippine Revolution of 1898, which would end the rule of Spain in the Philippines.

The arrival of the Americans

While Filipino revolutionaries were struggling to free themselves from the Spanish yoke, war broke out between Spain and the United States. Admiral Dewey met in Hong Kong with Emilio Aguinaldo, the exiled head of the Philippine Revolutionary Government, to negotiate the takeover of the Philippines. The Spaniards' pride made it too difficult to capitulate to the Filipino revolutionaries; instead, they surrendered to American troops after a mock battle* at Manila Bay. In the negotiations, from which Filipinos were totally excluded, the U.S. "bought" the Philippines for 20 million dollars.

The exclusion of the Filipinos from negotiation was particularly insulting because by June 12, 1898, Aguinaldo had declared independence from Spain, establishing an interim government that was designed to evolve into a representative government. This move provoked conflict between the Filipino troops and the occupying American army. The situation grew to critical proportions when, on December 21, 1898, the Tagalog version of McKinley's proclamation of "Benevolent Assimilation" appeared in public. This proclamation clearly indicated the American intention of staying permanently in the Philippines.

The tension finally snapped in a shooting incident at the San Juan Bridge. Again, the Filipinos found themselves struggling to be free, this time from a new aggressor. Fierce fighting lasted until 1902, when American military superiority put down the Filipinos' brave defense in a bloody conflict that cost many Filipino lives. As Constantino points out:

* There are varied accounts of this battle in which no one was killed. Stuart Creighton Miller, in his book *Benevolent Assimilation* (Yale University Press, 1982, p. 43), insists that it was a sham battle arranged to save the Spanish commander's reputation and rank, and that the few injuries on both sides were due to some "actors bungling their lines," or possibly to the fact that few officers were let in on the charade.

Figures on casualties and on economic losses for the whole country attest to the suffering inflicted by the suppression campaigns and are likewise indicators of the mass resistance the people waged. General Bell himself estimated that one-sixth of the population of Luzon had died as a result of the various campaigns to crush resistance. This would put the casualty figure at 600,000. Other authorities put the deaths directly caused by the war at 200,000. The economic plight of the survivors may be gleaned from the fact that 90 percent of the carabaos had died or had been slaughtered for food, and the rice harvest was down to one-fourth of the normal production level.[7]

During this time the Philippine Independent Church (also called "The Aglipayan Church") was founded by Isabelo de los Reyes, a journalist and labor leader, and by Gregorio Aglipay, chaplain to the Philippine Revolutionary Army. It was a church founded during the upsurge of nationalism that was part of the conflict between the Spanish friars and the native Filipino clergy.

This was also the time that the first American Protestant missionaries arrived under the banner of "Manifest Destiny."[*] The Americans brought with them the principle of the separation of church and state and a secular public education system.

During the early years of their rule, the Americans negotiated the sale of the "friar lands," church-owned lands that had caused much controversy. A unique opportunity for an equitable redistribution of land was lost when these lands were sold to the *caciques*, or private landowners.

"Free" trade initiated between the U.S. and the Philippines ushered in the modern era of the Philippines' economic dependency, as Nicholas Tarling aptly points out:

---

[*] See "A Philippine Protestant Chronology," page 160.

The vast expansion of exports that took place under the free trade system with the U.S. took place within the framework of existing social and economic patterns. If the new imperialism aimed at fostering political independence, it was bound to be qualified by economic dependence. If its objective was democracy, it was bound to be compromised by social inequality. The Filipinos were the first again to feel the problems that have more recently beset the "underdeveloped countries."[8]

Extended economic exploitation of a colony can occur only when people openly accept the colonial rule. To achieve this, the U.S. used a whole cultural structure, "Americanizing" Philippine society through public school education, by the use of English as the medium of instruction, and by sending many Filipino *pensionados* (persons supported by scholarships) to study in the United States. These programs had the effect of "dissipating the intense feeling of nationalism that had animated the Revolution and the resistance to American occupation."[9]

The Americanization of Philippine society was so successful that the U.S. could dangle before the people the promise of Philippine independence and a semblance of democracy, knowing that many Filipinos had come to accept the idea of independence as a "grant" from the United States.

Not all dissent was destroyed, however. Throughout the years of American occupation, a number of militant organizations were established. The first labor groups were founded, and peasants united to fight the evils of tenancy and usury. A popular protest movement called Sakdalism denounced the evils of colonialism. It was at this point that Communism was introduced into the Philippines; the Communist Party was formally established on November 7, 1930. It was outlawed by the Supreme Court in 1932.

Under American tutelage and under a new constitution, the Philippine Commonwealth was inaugu-

The Filipino People 17

rated on November 15, 1935. As described by the nationalist patriot Claro M. Recto:

> Our Constitution was frankly an imitation of the American charter. Many of the delegates were products of an American system of education and consequently were obsessed with the sincere belief that democracy could be defined only in American terms.[10]

The first president of the Commonwealth was Manuel L. Quezon.

The Philippines was once again plunged into bloody conflict with the outbreak of World War II. Japan, which belonged to the Axis powers, invaded the Philippines as a U.S. colony when the United States, joining the Allies, declared war on Germany. For the three years that the Filipinos were under Japanese rule they suffered the consequences of a war that was not theirs. President Quezon was heard to exclaim during a trying moment:

> Listen to what the shameless ones in Washington are saying...For thirty years I have worked and hoped for my people. Now they burn and die for a flag that could not protect them...How typically American to writhe in anguish at the fate of a distant cousin [England] while a daughter is being raped in the back room![11]

When Americans did arrive in 1944, they were hailed throughout the islands as liberators. The war ended with Manila in ruins.

The Philippines from 1946 to 1972

On July 4, 1946, High Commissioner Paul V. McNutt, representing President Harry Truman, read the following proclamation of Philippine independence:

> I do hereby recognize the independence of the Philippines as a separate and self-governing nation and acknowledge the authority and control over the same of the government instituted by the

people thereof under the Constitution now in force.[12]

The Philippines' new president was Manuel M. Roxas, who was responsible for the constitution's parity amendment, which gave Americans the same right as Filipinos to "dispose, exploit, develop and utilize all agricultural, timber and mineral lands in the Philippines together with the right to operate public utilities."[13]

The Philippines had become politically independent but remained economically dependent on the United States. It had thus entered that era called neocolonialism.

In the 1950s the government faced growing agrarian unrest. The Hukbalahaps, which began as an anti-Japanese resistance movement, was transformed into a communist armed group.

In 1953, Ramon Magsaysay was elected president on the basis of his effective campaign against the "Huks" while secretary of national defense. At the time he enjoyed the image of being the president of the common *tao*, but more recent critiques show him to have been a protégé of the United States. Under Magsaysay's administration, the Laurel-Langley agreement was established, revising the parity amendment to extend to Americans the right to engage in *all* business activities in the Philippines.* Magsaysay also ushered in a new era marked by the heavy use of U.S. "advisers" in the formulation of domestic and foreign policies.

The next president, Carlos Garcia (1957-1961), made efforts to steer the country towards a more independent economy by adopting a "Filipino First" policy and a policy of protectionism. But American pressure put an end to his efforts and in 1961, the U.S. supported his opponent, Diosdado Macapagal, who proclaimed his faith in free enterprise and promptly lifted exchange controls. Decontrol killed many budding industries in the Philippines and enabled foreign

---

* Amended in 1974 to prohibit Americans from owning land.

control of the economy to become even more deeply entrenched.

The economic crisis generated by Macapagal's policies became his undoing, and in 1965 Ferdinand E. Marcos was elected on the basis of what was considered a nationalistic platform. Marcos, however, chose to recommit the country to free enterprise and decontrol. He also sent Filipino troops to Vietnam, a decision that met with massive opposition and mass demonstrations, and allowed the U.S. military bases in the Philippines to be used for bombing sorties in Vietnam. These actions earned him the title "The U.S.'s Right-Hand Man in Asia." Marcos also introduced development programs via the so-called Nixon Doctrine, which consisted of U.S.-conceived aid programs and projects, especially in the agricultural sector.

By Marcos' second term, the logic of a dependent economy was following its inexorable course, causing a massive, uncontrollable outflow of dollars, which led to a balance of payment crisis. By June 1970, the Philippines had the highest inflation rate in the world.*

The economic crisis caused a new upsurge of mass movements with some new characteristics:

> These mass movements were more pronounced as the close of the sixties and opening of the seventies were qualitatively different from its predecessors. These movements were more articulate than the previous ones and were clearer and more coherent in their analysis, goals, and programs. The movement rolled behind the banner of "National Democracy" which regarded "the overthrowing of U.S. imperialism, feudalism and bureacratic capitalism and the seizure of political power and its consolidation for the liberation of the great masses of the Filipino people" in the present era as the central task of the Philippine revolution.[14]

---

* Subsequent inflation rates have been even higher.

In the face of this growing mass movement and on
the stated basis of "general breakdown of law and
order, the threat of a communist-led insurrection, and
the Muslim rebellion in the south," Marcos declared
martial law on September 21, 1972.

The martial law years, 1972 to 1986

The twenty years of the Marcos regime were marked
by one-man rule, by repression of civil liberties and
violations of human rights, by a worsening economic
crisis and dependency, and by corruption unprece-
dented in Philippine history, as shown in the
subsequent disclosures of the wealth amassed by the
Marcos family.

It was, however, a period of intense political
awakening. At no time in their history were the
Filipino people so politicized and mobilized as during
the martial law years, when activism brought with it
the risk of arrest, torture, detention, "salvaging"
(summary execution) and massacre.

The people organized according to their "sectors"
and national organizations emerged, made up of
peasants, workers, urban poor, teachers, students and
women. Claiming the history of struggle as their
legacy, these men and women fought for a vision of
a more egalitarian, more economically and politically
self-reliant and independent society.

At first, the movement was principally made up of
poor people and was primarily, if not exclusively,
initiated by "left leaning" or "cause-oriented" people's
organizations. With the assassination of Benigno
Aquino on August 21, 1983, however, the middle class
joined what Filipinos were calling "the parliament of
the streets."

In February 1986, in a memorable four-day event, a
military uprising with massive civilian support, the
Marcos regime ended. Corazon Cojuanco Aquino,
widow of Benigno Aquino, who was considered the
real winner of the presidential elections of February 6,

1986, assumed the task of being the first woman president of the Philippines.

The contemporary Philippines

Economy

The essential structure of the economic system in the Philippines has remained unchanged for the last fifty years. Two basic problems beset this system. First, there is the unequal distribution of resources, with 2 percent of the population owning and controlling 75 percent of the land and capital. The other problem is the foreign control of the economy.

The Philippines is still basically an agricultural economy. Its land is still cultivated chiefly under the tenancy system. Some plantations, however, have passed into the hands of transnational corporations engaging in agribusiness. Unfortunately, land reform programs before the Philippine congress at the time of this writing have been denounced by both landlords and farmers and are not likely to solve the country's fundamental land problems.

Compounding the problem of the unequal distribution of resources is foreign control of the economy. This continues through transnational corporations, which take their profits out of the country, and through the nation's indebtedness to the International Monetary Fund-World Bank (IMF-WB), which at the time of this writing was 28.58 billion dollars. This economic dependence, according to the economist Lichauco, is responsible for the failure of Philippine capitalism to launch industrialization. It condemns the Philippines to economic underdevelopment, which Lichauco describes as "a people's state of incapacity to produce their means of production." He explains:

> Private foreign capital, largely represented by transnational corporations, cannot possibly have an interest in seeing agricultural economy, which is markets for industrial products, transformed into industrial economy. The reason is that there

is a fundamental contradiction between the
interest of transnational corporations, on one
hand, and on the other, the interest of
underdeveloped economies striving toward
development.[15]

Hence:

In the very structure of our economy is the
fundamental explanation for our mass poverty.
Until the structure is changed through the
emergence and development of a dynamic
industrial base, the masses cannot hope to be
relieved of their misery. Not even the massive
application of palliatives will relieve them of that
misery. They have been recipients of palliatives for
the last thirty years. And they will continue to be
miserable until this country finally moves from
the pre-industrial to the industrial age.[16]

All of this has caused thousands of Filipinos to leave
the country to earn their living. Skilled male workers
go to countries like Saudi Arabia. Filipino women,
mostly high school graduates but oftentimes professionals, go to the cities of Asia, Europe and the United
States, finding work usually as domestics and
entertainers. Not a few women have escaped the
economic crisis by resorting to the "mail-order bride"
system popular in such countries as New Zealand,
Australia and West Germany.

Politics

Ferdinand Marcos' twenty-year regime ended
quickly in February 1986 following grossly fraudulent
elections. The collapse was a result of complex forces
precipitated by military defections and made possible
by the awesome political force of masses of Filipinos
expressing themselves nonviolently in the streets, by
the strong encouragement of Roman Catholic church
leaders, and by the abrupt shift of U.S. policy (and
behind-the-scenes activity) to favor the ousting of
Marcos.

While most would agree that something truly remarkable happened in the Philippines, it is unwise to be overly preoccupied with the "People's Power Revolution" and the change of rule, since basic economic and political reform has not yet taken place. Corazon C. Aquino took her oath of office on February 26, 1986. Democratic forms have been reintroduced. A new constitution has been promulgated and a new bicameral congress has been elected. However, the situation is still rather unstable. The military is divided and no significant part of it is totally under the control of the new administration. In August 1987, an unprecedentedly bloody right-wing coup attempt claimed fifty-three lives. Law and order have largely broken down and there is a proliferation of armed civilians. Vigilante groups have been sanctioned by the administration and private armies have been raised to protect vested interests.* Far from solving the problem, the government's anti-insurgency program has caused the escalation of violence both in the countryside and in the urban areas. This is to be expected, since poverty and injustice, the roots of insurgency, have not yet been squarely faced.

At the time of this writing, there has been no real change, either in the political structure or in the class of people who are the nation's rulers. Hence, the same interests are being protected, including those of the U.S. In fact, the United States' influence in the Philippines has never been more overt nor more pervasive than it is at present. Political analysts have identified in the Philippines manifestations of strategies of Low Intensity Conflict (LIC) similar to those the U.S. has put into use in Central America.

Meanwhile, nationalists and people's organizations continue in their struggle to deal with the basic issues still confronting the country. They are having a hard time positioning themselves, due to the intensive "Red

---

* A majority block in the Philippine senate has passed a resolution calling for the dismantling of the vigilante groups. Many are worried, however, that other types of armed groups may take their place.

scare" (anti-communist) campaigns of both the state and the church.

Culture

With a history that looks back through four hundred and fifty years of Western colonialism, it is inevitable that Filipinos' culture has been marked by Western influence. As has been noted, Spain's main contribution to Filipino culture was Christianity. The fiestas, processions and colorful pageants of traditional Filipino Catholicism bear a striking resemblance to the celebrations and processions of Sevilla. Filipinos have not quite given up their traditional beliefs and cults. Many still superimpose certain Christian rituals on their own practices and cults. As the sociologist-educator Onofre Corpuz writes:

> ... Filipino folk Christianity reconciles in one system the rigid monotheism of Christian dogma alongside of belief in a world of minor deities that solicitously guard over dwellings, trees, rivers, straits, fields, and forests.[17]

Describing how such syncretism develops, sociologist Agaton Pal gives examples of the way animistic and Christian traditions are combined in prayers to patron saints:

> Thus since San Pedro is the saint of the fishermen, a fisherman hoping for aid may light a candle to San Pedro but his actions to appease the spirit do not stop with the traditional Catholic action, for he floats a raft on the water loaded with eggs, chicken or tuba as a sacrifice to the spirit of the water. Likewise farmers offer prayers to San Isidro, their patron saint, but also place drink and saltless food at the edge of the field as an offering to the pre-Christian spirit. Households with sick members similarly pray to a patron saint and also hire an herbolario to propitiate the spirits suspected of having caused the illness.[18]

There are many "modern" Filipinos, of course, whom this description does not fit. There is a world of difference between the culture of the urban Filipino and that of the rural Filipino. And there is absolutely no doubt that the prevailing urban culture is "American" in many aspects, from tastes in clothing and entertainment to the school system, curricula and the language of instruction.

But whether they live in urban or rural areas, Filipinos hold similar values—for example, the high priority placed on a close-knit family. The study on social acceptance made by the noted sociologist Fr. Frank Lynch applies to both rural and urban Filipinos. This includes the value of *pakikisama* ("good public relations," or camaraderie); the use of go-betweens to settle conflicts; the importance of *hiya* (shame) and "keeping face"; and the sense of *amor propio*, or self-esteem, which is shown in Filipinos' "sensitivity to personal affront."[19]

Likewise, sociologist Mary Hollensteiner's study of reciprocity holds true for city and village folks alike. This includes the importance of the *utang na loob* (debt of gratitude), the giving of *abuloy* (contributions to those in need), and *bayanihan* (cooperative work).[20]

Fr. Jaime Bulatao's study on the value system of Manileños (residents of Manila) is applicable to inhabitants of the provinces as well. The results of this study point out the value of emotional closeness and family security, the need for the approval of an authority, the importance of preserving tradition, the value of education for social mobility, the necessity of suffering before gaining happiness, and the need for religion and prayer as refuge in times of distress.[21]

Filipino hospitality is proverbial. When visitors, even uninvited ones, drop by during lunch or dinner time, they are invited to join the meal—not a usual practice in Western countries. A rural family will kill its last chicken to serve a guest. It is not farfetched to consider whether this trait, taken to the extreme, is in part responsible for the Philippines' unconditional "hospitality" to foreign transnational corporations, to the detriment of its own economy.

Filipino languages and dialects have assimilated up to twenty percent of their words from Castilian, the "purest" form of the Spanish language. These words appear here and there in daily speech. They talk of "tasa" (from *taza*, or cup), "bintana" (from *ventana*, or window), "kutsilyo" (*cuchillo*, or knife), "kutsara" (*cuchara*, or spoon), "silya" (*silla*, or chair), etc. Especially in urban areas and among the middle class, interjections such as "pero" (but), "sigue" (continue) and "terrible" punctuate conversations.

Spanish machismo seems to have influenced Filipinos' man-woman relationships, modifying the more egalitarian relationships that existed in the pre-colonial Philippines. Thus a wife is expected to keep the marriage intact no matter what her husband might do. A woman is supposed to forgive an unfaithful husband and is expected to continue to live with a wife-beating husband "for the sake of the children." There is a remarkable tolerance for the double standard of morality in favor of the male. It must be said, however, that the women's movement that has bloomed in the latter half of the 1980s has captured Filipinos' imagination, and women have organized themselves to remedy their situation. The largest of these women's groups is called GABRIELA.

In recent decades, with the awakening of the Filipino political awareness, efforts have been made—especially by people's organizations—to inculcate a national consciousness. Pilipino, which is based on the Tagalog language, has been designated as the national language; in 1988 it replaced English as the offical language of the government, and efforts are under way to make Pilipino a medium of instruction in the social sciences. Plays, dramas and movies consistently choose indigenous themes. More Filipino heroes, writers, composers and artists are studied in schools. However, the colonial mentality still prevails. There is thus a continuing effort to enable a national identity to evolve while assimilating into a meaningful whole the varied cultural heritage of the Filipino people.

NOTES

1. Teodoro Agoncillo. *A Short History of the Philippines* (Philippine Graphic Arts Inc., 1975), p. 22.
2. C.F. Pedro Paterno. *La Antiqua Civilizacion* (Madrid: Tipografia de Manuel E. Fernandez, 1987).
3. Mary John Mananzan. "A History of the Church in the Philippines," in *Asia and Christianity* (Bombay: Himalaya Publishing House, 1985), p. 57.
4. Teodoro Agoncillo, *op. cit.*, pp. 38-39.
5. Renato Constantino. *A Past Revisited* (Quezon City: Tala Publishing Services, 1975), p. 82.
6. Ibid., p. 82.
7. Ibid., p. 345.
8. Nicolas Tarling. *Southeast Asia* (Singapore: Donald Moore Press, Ltd., 1967), p. 200.
9. Renato Constantino, *op. cit.*, p. 308.
10. Claro M. Recto, quoted in Teodoro Agoncillo, *op. cit.*, p. 193.
11. Quoted in Teodoro Agoncillo, *op. cit.*, p. 241.
12. Ibid., p. 255.
13. Ibid., p. 254.
14. Mario Bolasco and Rolando Yu. *Church-State Relations* (Manila: St. Scholastica's College, 1981),   p. 46.
15. Alejandro Lichauco. *Towards a New Economic Order and the Conquest of Mass Poverty* (Manila, 1986), p. 20.
16. Ibid., pp. 12-13.
17. Onofre Corpuz. *The Philippines* (N.J. Presidential, 1976), p. 5.
18. Irene Ortigas Felix Regalado. *Society and Culture in the Rural Philippines* (Manila: Alemars Phoenix Publishing Co., 1978), p. 74.
19. Frank Lynch. "Social Acceptance," in *Four Readings in Philippine Values*, ed. by Frank Lynch (Quezon City: Ateneo de Manila University Press, 1968), pp. 1-21.
20. Mary Hollensteiner. "Reciprocity," in Lynch, *Four Readings, op. cit.*, pp. 22-49.
21. Jaime Bulatao. "The Manileño's Mainsprings," in Lynch, *Four Readings, op. cit.*, pp. 50-56.

Editors' Note

In a country where about seventy percent of the people are poor, one might expect that a "church of the poor" would evolve naturally. The fact is, after more than four hundred years of Christianity, this has only come about in the last two decades. But now the poor in the Philippines are making the church their own in a very special way.

One of the biggest factors in this change is the emergence of Basic Christian Communities (BCC's). From its beginnings within traditional parish patterns that focused almost solely on liturgical activities, prayer and religious celebrations, the BCC movement has grown to integrate Christian faith and organized action.

Small groups of Christians come together to reflect on the Bible and the pressing issues they face in their lives. The theological question centers on the meaning of the gospel: "What is the good news? What is good about it? For whom is it good?"

> What is good news to a worker in a Caloocan factory who eats only twice a day and breaks his back for eight hours of hard work to earn a measly thirteen pesos or less? What is good news to a farmer in Nueva Ecija planting onion seedlings imported from the United States and Japan whose cost of production places him in an endless cycle of debt? What is good news to a fisherman in a subdivision lake controlled by big Japanese trawlers? Or to the tribal Filipinos driven from their ancestral homes to give way to multinational companies in the name of progress?[*]

In the past, the poor tended to accept their lot unquestioningly, seeing it as their assigned fate. Now they ask questions and show new convictions about

---

[*] From *Moving Heaven and Earth*, WCC Commission on the Churches' Participation in Development (CCPD), 1982.

things like justice, God's sovereignty and human responsibility. One of the important components of the BCC movement has been the training of lay leaders for liturgical functions and for the churches' "total development programs" in such areas as community health, cooperatives, literacy work and agricultural production projects. Priests and nuns began to live among the people in urban slums. They provided support for labor organizing and were active advocates for people's housing needs. They encouraged people to actively seek change.

It did not take very long before the Basic Christian Communities were seen as a threat to established power—at that time, that of the Marcos regime. Many Basic Christian Community leaders have suffered as a result. Many were harassed in various ways, some were killed and others have disappeared.

Bishop Julio X. Labayen, O.C.D., author of the chapter that begins this section, is the bishop of a region of the Philippines that is economically very poor. He has witnessed first hand the poverty and deprivation of his flock, including the atrocities they suffer (even though Marcos is gone) as a consequence of the militarization of the area. We ask readers to keep this background in mind as they read this chapter.

THE CHURCH OF THE POOR

Julio Xavier Labayen, O.C.D.

It is my conviction that if the Bible were being written today, it would be about some poor people's struggle for a homeland in a small country of little note to us. The inspired writers would describe God's love for this people and their leaders and would find God's hand in all that happened to them, good or bad. Little would be said about the superpowers, no more than was said about Rome and Egypt in the Bible. Little would be said about the superpowers' problems or priorities, their visions or ideologies, their sense of destiny.

In the Philippines, we who opt to stand with the poor do so not because the poor are better than the rich; nor because they are holy and the rich are not; much less because they are the majority. We believe that we are simply following God's lead and example. But to take up the struggle on the side of the poor is to put oneself in a risky and controversial position.

In our society, in which the rich and the powerful dominate and rule, the question is raised: "What about the rich? Why such a fuss about the poor? Does not God love both the rich and the poor? Did not Jesus Christ die for both the rich and the poor? Is it not God's will to save everybody?"

With the building up of anti-Communist hysteria and anti-Marxist propaganda in our society today, we are often asked: "Is this orientation to the poor not a veiled

Julio X. Labayen, a Carmelite priest, is bishop of the prelature "Nullius" of Infanta, Quezon Province. He was formerly the director of the Roman Catholic National Secretariat for Social Action, and chaired the Office for Human Development of the Federation of Asian Bishops Conferences.

strategy to promote class struggle? What will happen
to society if you eliminate the rich? How can the poor
run the country or develop society? Doesn't
Christianity preach reconciliation and unity?" Or we
hear the remarks: "The church is unwittingly allowing
itself to be used by the Communists," or, "The Church
of the Poor is simply a front, a cover for Communist
activity." Those who stand with the poor in our country
are discredited and branded as disgruntled elements:
"subversives," "leftists," "Marxists," "Communists"!

What is the truth about the Church of the Poor?
This chapter attempts to proclaim that truth.

Discovering the Church of the Poor

The first time I came across the phrase "the Church
of the Poor" was in a document from the first Asian
bishops' meeting in Manila in November 1970. The late
Pope Paul VI presided over this historic and significant
meeting.

God is calling the churches in Asia to become the
Church of the Poor.

The Asian bishops, in plenary assembly, came to this
conclusion after scrutinizing the signs of the times
across the vast Asian continent and interpreting them
in the light of the Gospel of Jesus Christ.

It is our resolve, first of all, to be more truly the
Church of the Poor. If we are to place ourselves at
the side of the multitudes in our continent, we
must in our way of life share something of their
poverty. The Church cannot set up islands of
affluence in a sea of want and misery; our own
personal lives must give witness to *evangelical*
simplicity, and no man, no matter how lowly or
poor, should find it hard to come to us and find
in us their brothers. (*Message of the Asian Bishops.*
29 November 1970, Manila)

In 1968, in Medellin, Colombia, our brother bishops
in Latin America had already stated a *preferential option*

for the poor. In the process of updating their pastoral orientation according to the guidelines of Vatican II, they felt that a disciple of Jesus Christ is called upon to take the side of the poor in today's world.

My understanding leads me to think that this option, if we take it, is as full of unforeseen, profound consequences for the church and for us bishops as was the decision of the early Christians to leave their orientation toward Jewish traditions and venture into the Graeco-Roman world.

Some of the Christians back then in Jerusalem probably sensed that there was more at stake than a few prescriptions of Mosaic law, but they had no way of knowing what their choice would mean for the church and for human history. How could they have imagined their descendants in the faith discussing Christ the Lord in very theoretical terms, or that a series of church councils would be called to define Christian dogma? They forged ahead because they believed that Jesus was Lord and that all peoples should have access to Him. They definitely understood the Lord's injunction: "Go out to the whole world: proclaim the Good News to all creation" (Mark 16:16). It was the great ecclesiological decision of history!

The effect on the life of the present-day Christian church of a decision to side with the poor would be of similar magnitude. It would affect every aspect of our lives. How, and how deeply, we cannot now comprehend. Yet we are called to make such a decision for a host of reasons—religious, sociological, historical, political. These reasons amass one upon the other. But finally, the option for the poor is taken less as a reasoned conclusion than as *a basic act of faith*. It is the option that Jesus took. As followers in his footsteps we take the same option. Taking it, we sense we have "come home."

Discerning the presence of God among the poor

The overriding reason we are for the poor is because God is with them. God, and God's Christ, have already

taken the option. My friend Father Samuel Rayan, an
Indian Jesuit theologian, put it this way:

> It is in the struggle of the poor that God speaks
> and reveals Himself. That is the stand the Bible
> takes. It is different from the Constantinian idea
> that God is in the wars of the rich. The privilege
> of the poor, then, is not a national or social factor;
> it is not even a moral factor. The poor are not
> privileged on the basis of race or virtue or learning.
> They are dear to God because they are victims
> of the system, reduced to nothing, underdevel-
> oped by the mighty. (1 Corinthians 1:26-31; Mark
> 12:10-12)
>
> They are elected, and the Word is addressed to
> them. So they stand close to God and organize
> the struggle. They, and God through them, are
> now inviting us to conversion. (*Vidyajyoti*. March,
> 1982)

As I have said, we opt for the poor not because they
are better, holier or more numerous than the rich. We
simply believe that we are following God's lead and
example.

Perhaps this act of faith in seeking God's presence
in the lives and struggles of the poor will be as difficult
for us as it was for Thomas or Nicodemus to discern
the God of the Covenant in a mortal man whose name
was Jesus of Nazareth!

While there are sociological reasons for siding with
the poor (poor people's participation in decision-
making has been advocated even by the United Nations
General Assembly), for Christians, the option for the
poor is, at bottom, the option of Jesus. Father James
Carney, an American Jesuit believed to have been killed
by the Honduras military in September 1983, wrote:

> The poor Christian peasants of Honduras have
> opened the Gospel for me. I did not know the
> real Jesus—the peasant of Nazareth—until I
> reflected on the Bible with the peasant Christian
> leaders here. I did not understand anything of the

humble life of Mary—the peasant woman of
Nazareth—until I contemplated the Honduran
peasant women cutting firewood and carrying it
home on their heads to cook with.

Father Carney is telling us that we must learn from
the poor. We must sit at their feet not so much to know
what tenet or doctrine to believe, but to understand
what to value in life and how to act as Christians who
are concerned about a full human life for all.

Taking the point of view of the poor

Some theologians and pastors tell us it is the poor who
will teach us about the God of Jesus Christ—that it
is *they* who will evangelize *us*. But what does this mean?

It means that we learn to look at the world, its present
reality and its history, through the eyes of the poor,
particularly the poor who have opened their eyes to
their own dignity, destiny and responsibility and are
prepared to do something about it. These are the people
we sometimes refer to as "the organized poor."

I am not equating the worldview of the poor with
the "correct" view. Much less am I saying it is the "mind
of Christ." There is sin and ignorance among the poor,
of course!

What I am saying is that the aspiration for a more
just, more human, more compassionate and familial
world resounds more urgently and sharply from the
hearts of people who have deeply and continuously
experienced what it means to be the dehumanized
victims of systematic avarice and greed.

Affirming the participation of the poor and standing with them

Unless we wish to be the pharaohs of today, we must
allow the poor to act as God inspires them to take
part in decisions that affect their lives and their future.
This holds true for life in the wider society as well
as in the church.

Our Basic Christian Communities, born of our faith that God is among the poor, provide mechanisms that help people play a more active role in important decision-making. Similar mechanisms abound in poor people's organizations. We encourage the growth of these people's groups and we walk with them in their struggle to become architects of their own history and destiny.

The Asian and Latin American bishops have been inspired to proclaim the Good News that the kingdom is being realized here and now. As reflected in the Asian bishops' 1970 statement, their aspiration is *to make a preferential option for the poor, and to become the Church of the Poor.*

Yet such a thrust is today overshadowed by the loud voices and effective propaganda of the rich and the powerful, and by the "priests" of the world economic order. In place of worship of the true God, they offer for worship the "golden calf" of wealth, power and prestige.

But when people organize themselves for the struggle to liberate themselves from a system that oppresses, exploits and represses them, they are considered a threat to the established order and to those who hold power. And so such organizations are often misrepresented as directly endangering the security of the state.

In order to legitimize military and police action that resists the struggles of the poor, recourse is made to the ideology of national state security. From our experience under martial law, we notice that the state, supposedly composed of people, territory and government, is reduced to mean only the government. Thus the government, buttressed by its military force, assumes the right to defend and protect "the established order" against its people. And, ironically, the people become its victims. The system is thus idolized, made the ultimate value. And people and territory are oftentimes sacrificed to appease this idol.

To justify actions against the organized poor, the powers that be conveniently invoke the East-West confrontation between the two superpowers, the USA and the Soviet Union, the confrontation between "atheistic communism" and "materialistic capitalism." Those who protest against capitalism are accused of being on the side of communism, and vice versa. It is a fact that this confrontation gave birth to the arms race and to the policy of deterrence, or Mutual Assured Destruction (MAD). It has given rise to a national security ideology, to militarism as a new philosophy of government that sees preparedness for war as the way to stability and peace. "If you want peace, prepare for war!"

Peace is thus seen as the result of a precarious balance between horrendous arsenals of nuclear death. Peace is understood to be merely the absence of war. But our experience in the Philippines tells us that even in the absence of war there is no peace. Peasants continue to be restive because of unsettled agrarian problems. Industry is plagued with strikes because of the unanswered clamor of workers for fair labor conditions. True peace can only be the fruit of an order where social justice prevails and the common good is a reality.

Well did Pope John Paul II declare in his message for the World Day of Prayer for Peace on January 2, 1985: "Peace is a value with no frontiers: east-west, north-south, only one peace." Peace must be viewed not only from the one-sided perspective of the East-West military confrontation, but likewise from the perspective of the relationship of injustice between the powerful and the weak, the rich and the poor. The way to genuine and lasting peace is the way of justice, not of militarism.

The church that takes the side of the struggling poor and shares in their struggle for liberation from an oppressive system inevitably shares the blows that secure the system. Like Jesus, the Church of the Poor hears and understands God's will in the context of the struggles of the poor. Following the footprints of its Founder, Leader and Lord, Jesus Christ, it walks the path of poverty and persecution.

We are challenged

Today, a large number of the poor in Asia and in the other third-world continents have awakened to the violence done to their human dignity and to the violations committed against their human rights. They are rising up to free themselves from the wanton acts and oppressive systems that condemn them to poverty, misery, despair, fatalism and colonial dependence.

How do we in the church look at their struggle for liberation? Do we conveniently rationalize our non-commitment by saying that we must stay out of politics? The issues of poverty and injustice, whichever way we look at them, are political issues, and we cannot escape them.

Should liberation from sin be concerned solely with individual sin in the human heart? Should it not also be concerned with collective sin and liberation from its results, structural and systemic?

There are three things for us to remember when we take the option for the poor:

First, we in the middle class, including bishops like myself, must admit that our perspective is different from that of the poor. As long as this is so, we can hardly empathize with the urgency and sharpness of their aspiration for a just, humane and compassionate society. Our tendency is to fall into detached conversation about the problems of the poor, to form committees to study them, to make plans that do not enjoy a high priority and to dilly-dally in implementing them, then to taking comfort in the thought that at least we have done something for the poor.

Second, we have to be open to listening and learning from the poor. We are often tempted to think that we have little or nothing to learn from them, or that their ignorance makes them easy prey to communists who will manipulate them. This is exactly the same attitude assumed by dictatorial governments towards their poor people.

Third, we can do no less than take the same attitude as that of Jesus Christ the Evangelist, the bearer of

Good News: to be open to all possibilities and forms of the coming of God's kingdom in concrete situations and in the ongoing historical process. In doing so, we place our full trust and hope in the God of the Covenant, whose dream for God's people is frustrated in the actual plight of the poor, the hungry and the afflicted. We manifest Christ's spirit of poverty when we embrace a simple lifestyle for the sake of the kingdom. This voluntary poverty ensures compassion, mercy, equitable sharing, passion for truth, justice, freedom and unselfish love.

The Church of the Poor understands the true dynamics of violence in the politics of this world. It holds that in the long run, it is not physical force, but the triumph of dialogue, justice, truth and freedom that will bring about genuine and lasting peace.

The Church of the Poor is the church that offers, along with Jesus Christ, continuing praise and thanksgiving to God in the firm hope that the power of the risen Lord is active in history and that life, not death, will have the final word.

Thy kingdom come!

EMERGING SHAPES AND FORMS IN ECUMENISM

Notes from the Philippine Experience

LaVerne D. Mercado

The ecumenical movement has affirmed from its inception that what it is about is not confined to adjusting or repairing relationships among churches, but that its most important work has to to do with the relationship between the church and the world. For many Christians around the world this has meant, iterally, being present at the "bleeding points of history" and, in such contexts, coming face to face with the pressure-points of the transformation of church and society. This point of view has indeed characterized the ecumenical enterprise in the Philippines in the past several years and I would like to suggest that it will continue to do so in the years ahead.

The Second Vatican Council sounded out the meaning of this ecumenism in its now-famous declaration on the pastoral action of the church in the world:

The joys and the hopes, the griefs and the anxieties of the men of this age, especially those who are poor or in any way afflicted, these are the joys

LaVerne D. Mercado, elected a bishop of the United Methodist Church in the Philippines in 1976, was general secretary of the National Council of Churches in the Philippines (NCCP) from 1973 to 1987, a most difficult period of the Marcos era, during which a number of NCCP staff were arrested and held without charges. He himself was held in detention for a period of time.

and hopes, the griefs and anxieties of the followers
of Christ. Indeed, nothing genuinely human fails
to raise an echo in their hearts. (*Gaudium et Spes.*
Section 1)

We cannot say that we have been particularly
innovative while others have stuck to the well-trod
paths of the past. And we cannot say that we have
acted in novel and peculiar ways. We do say, however,
that in assuming and identifying with the "joys and
the hopes, the griefs and anxieties of the men [and
women]" of our given time and place, "especially those
who are poor and in any way afflicted," we have
discovered some new and vibrant forms of ecumenical
relations that we had not touched upon before. We
have also discovered, in the process, new forms of what
it means to be the church in the world. Let me briefly
describe some of the discoveries.

Companions together in the people's struggle

The affliction that had fallen upon us was that of martial
rule brought about by the dictatorial Marcos regime.
Amid the rapacity of this regime, amid the untold
suffering it brought to people and to the whole of
Philippine society, amid its violations of human rights
and emasculation of people's welfare, amid the
incredible sacrifice of the patrimony of the nation in
favor of the sudden wealth of a selected few, and amid
the sweeping decay and destruction of cherished
democratic institutions and practices, we discovered
a common task in which joint action of Christians had
to take place. That task is what a Roman Catholic
practitioner of the "new" Catholic spirituality calls the
difficult but redemptive discovery of the church as
"partner, participant and companion of the people's
struggle, of the people's march to the kingdom."

This discovery is difficult because the church has
been accustomed to being "lord and teacher" of people
even in their struggles. It requires, therefore, no less
than a conversion on the church's part. This is
redemptive for the church because in the process it

has recovered its authentic servant role, recognizing that it stands and works not alone, but with others. The church's eyes have at last been opened to the fact that people who suffer are the subjects of their own social redemption. In the process, Christians have rediscovered the fact that the central content of Christian spirituality is the imperative for justice. They have also experienced a new context in which they encounter the give-and-take, the mutuality of contribution and the correction of ecumenism.

This discovery was not made in the seclusion of theological retreats, important as these have been. On the contrary, it was experienced concretely on the battlefronts of people's struggles. It was discovered, for example, as Christians from various confessions and denominations, laypeople, pastors, priests and nuns, helped to strengthen picket lines in workers' strikes; in people's marches where members of religious orders served as marshals; in the "parliament of the streets" where the Eucharist became a people's meal and provided them with equipment and power on the journey to freedom; in involvement with "cause-oriented groups" that gave vent to people's grievances and aspirations; and in that outpouring of "people's power" that brought down the Marcos regime, during which prayer and Bible study became a common platform of social protest.

In such contexts of companionship with people in their struggles, a Catholic nun might find reasons for saying, "I am a Protestant worker," and a Protestant pastor could say, "I am a Catholic religious." This by no means indicates that doctrinal and theological differences are glossed over by activism. It does mean that a common context is experienced where the grounds for mutual understanding and mutual commitments are forged. From such experiences new ecumenical configurations are being born and will continue to live.

Tentmakers and sanctuaries

In the recent life of the National Council of Churches in the Philippines (NCCP) this ecumenical companionship in the people's struggle has been given credence by the testimony of people from two crucial sectors of Philippine society. During a consultation on the image and self-understanding of the NCCP, a well-known peasant leader pointed out the fact that at one of the major mass actions of the peasant movement, staff members of the council cancelled their Christmas party and donated their Christmas meal as food for the peasant marchers. When the peasants camped in one of the open parks of the city, the Council provided the tents in which the marchers slept. These symbolic acts, the peasant leader concluded, are but small part of the greater solidarity and support which the Council has been giving to the peasant movement through the years, and no history of the peasant movement could be written without the Council being a prominent part of it.

During the same consultation, a leader from one of the largest labor unions testified to the fact that during the dark days of the Marcos regime, when hardly anyone dared to give support to the militant labor movement, "this compound where the NCCP is located," he said, "has been a constant sanctuary for workers who were being subjected to the repressive measures of the Marcos military. This is a matter which the labor movement in the country will never forget."

Though not of the peasant movement nor of the labor movement, the Council, in its companionship with them, along with other Christian groups that have engaged in similar acts of solidarity and support, is part of that larger fellowship of suffering people on their journey to freedom and greater well-being. In the process, it embodies a broad ecumenism of partnership and participation that not only cuts across confessional boundaries but goes beyond ecclesiastical frontiers into the larger struggle for the peace, unity and justice of the whole human family. It is an ecumenism rooted in the affirmation that people's struggle for freedom and justice is integral to the proclamation of the gospel of Jesus Christ and to the unity and renewal of the church.

Ecumenism at the grassroots

What all of this has meant to the life of the Council is too significant and far-reaching to discuss adequately in a brief chapter. One result, however, is worth sharing. It has been felt that in order to take this broader and more popular ecumenism more seriously, and to deepen its roots, it is necessary to bring it closer to the levels of local church life.

Thus the Council has embarked upon a process of regionalizing its life and structure so that the challenge of ecumenical fellowship and action is brought into the life of local congregations and local situations. It is our hope that in bringing about encounters of churches "in each place," to use the phrase of the New Delhi Assembly of the World Council of Churches, we are also creating occasions where churches not only get to know one another more concretely, but also encounter in more real terms the sufferings and hopes of people everywhere and "in each place."

There are now Regional Ecumenical Committees in all the major regions of the country. In the brief time in which these regional groupings of churches have existed, we have already received greater sharpness of social awareness and certainly a greater inter-confessional fellowship at the grassroots. We think that from experience at the grassroots, from engagement in common action and from companionship with the struggles of people for greater well-being, we are helping to build not only the foundations of a new society but also creating the ingredients for a new and renewed church.

What, indeed, of the future?

It is not possible for us to predict what the future will bring either to our society or to our churches. We think,

nevertheless, that it is important for us to sow the seeds
and prepare the ground out of which a new blossoming
of faith can emerge, and out of which a new church
can grow and give continuous companionship on the
continuing march of our people towards a new order
of peace, prosperity, justice and freedom. This, we think,
is what ecumenism really means: a transformed and
continually transforming church in a transformed and
equally transforming society where people can live in
peace, enjoy the benefits of justice and prosperity, and
breathe the air of a free and compassionate society.

PHILIPPINE PROTESTANTISM

An Appreciative but Critical Reflection

Oscar S. Suarez

The Christian churches in the Philippines, Catholic and Protestant, are among the most visible vestiges of the nation's colonial history. Historians tell us that while the churches in the Philippines have grown to be the largest Christian community in all of Asia, they would not have taken such deep rootage and gained their large number of adherents had early Christian crusades stood apart from the colonial powers.

It may be seen as unfair to credit colonial conquest with the birth and growth of the Philippine Protestant churches, considering the labors of the American missionaries who began the work at the turn of the century. Indeed, mention must be made of their dedication and zeal, not only in organizing converts from Catholicism into small Protestant congregations and in pressing for a strict moral ethic, but also in their work among Tribal Filipinos, in the establishment of schools and hospitals, and in their training of native people for local clerical work. Among the direct outcome of that early missionary activity are some of today's best-known Protestant institutions such as Silliman University, Central Philippine University, Philippine Christian University and Mary Johnston Hospital, as well as such large Manila churches as Ellinwood Malate

Oscar S. Suarez, a minister of the United Church of Christ in the Philippines, was formerly pastor of the Church of the Risen Lord, University of the Philippines. He is currently doing doctoral studies at Princeton Theological Seminary.

Church and Knox and Central United Methodist
Churches.

The good will and diligence of the missionaries in
their Christian endeavors left an indelible imprint in
the hearts and minds of evangelical Filipinos.[1] Various
Protestant churches and individual members continue
today to nurture their long attachment to the American
missionaries, and in fact have always cherished their
return after home leaves or retirement. A good number
of local congregations treasure memorable moments
of missionary history and have named their churches
after missionaries who either pioneered work of
membership recruitment and organization or who
served as ministers among them for many years. As
far as the Protestant community in the Philippines is
concerned, missionaries were probably the most
appreciated representatives of the American colonial
regime.

"Manifest destiny" collides with Filipino aspirations

It must be pointed out, however, that the missionaries'
initial conception of their work in the Philippines was
not necessarily independent of the interests of the
American political leaders at the turn of the century
who saw the Philippine islands as a colony. In fact,
the thought of undertaking a Protestant crusade in the
Philippines came at a time when American nationalism
was the guiding force in continental expansion. It was
a time when American public opinion seemed more
slanted toward a truly aggressive foreign policy which
led, eventually, to the addition of new states to the
growing American republic. In the minds of most U.S.
leaders and prominent citizens was the belief in
"Manifest Destiny,"[2] or the idea of a divine mandate
to expand and wield power beyond the North American
continent.

Thus in 1898 when news of Commodore Dewey's
victory[3] over the Spanish naval fleet in Manila Bay hit
the headlines of American dailies, enthusiasm to take
the Philippines as a colony immediately dominated

debates and exchanges not only among U.S. political leaders but in the religious community as well. When evangelical groups in the U.S. began to promote Protestant mission in the islands, they explicitly justified the colonization program hurriedly being launched by the U.S. Government. An editorial in a Methodist paper was quoted as saying that

> We are no longer compelled to go to a foreign country to seek raw heathen. When patriotism and evangelism can go hand in hand, the one strengthens the other. If it should result that the Philippine islands are to remain under a protectorate of this country for years to come, it will be our immediate duty to establish a mission there. And how glorious it would be to think that we have one mission in the heathen world with the starry flag afloat above it![4]

Although most pronouncements were expressed largely in religious language, many evangelical leaders' strong support of colonization revealed what may be called the political side of the "missionary project" in the Philippines. Austin Phelps of Andover Seminary reportedly told an audience in the U.S.:

> Americans should look on these United States as first and foremost the chosen seat of enterprise for the world's conversion. Forecasting the future of Christianity, as statesmen forecast the destiny of nations, we must believe that it will be what the future of this country is to be. As goes America, so goes the world, in all that is vital to its mortal welfare.[5]

Few, if any, of the missionaries seriously took note of the bitter opposition among Filipinos to the United States' colonization of the Philippines. The truth was that even before the Philippine-American war broke out, Filipino revolutionaries had practically defeated Spain and had painstakingly prepared to establish an independent republic. In an effort to create the impression that U.S. assistance was indispensable to the rehabilitation and development of Philippine society, it was not openly acknowledged to the greater American public that Filipino resistance to American rule was broad and fierce. In fact, historians recount that the war between Filipinos and the U.S. lasted for years and claimed hundreds of thousands of Filipino lives. Historian Renato Constantino notes that because of the wide resistance of Filipinos to American rule, some 126,000 American troops had to be utilized in the war of suppression.[6]

The question then becomes: how did the missionaries articulate the relevance of the gospel to every human situation without dealing with an issue that meant life and death for Filipinos? To be sure, as predominant theological tradition dictates, evangelism and conversion to Christianity were the primary intents of the missionaries. Socio-political questions, therefore, took a back seat. But only after raising serious issues deeply rooted in the past can we properly begin to explore the ministry, past and present, of the Protestant community in the Philippines.

The "missionary project" and the rise of Philippine Protestantism

Records show that the earliest foreign Protestant missionary activity in the Philippines goes back to the late 1800s, when the American Bible Society made attempts to smuggle Bibles into the country. During the same years, Protestant Spanish ministers reportedly sneaked into the islands intending to distribute Bibles in Spanish and Pangasinan translations.[7]

Large-scale mission work, however, began in 1898 with the American occupation, at almost exactly the same time that the Philippine-American war broke out. Among the first mission groups to arrive were the Methodists, Presbyterians and Episcopalians, who, according to some accounts, made dramatic numerical gains in just a few years. Even today, they (and their successors) are the largest evangelical groups in the country. (In 1948 the Presbyterians, Congregationalists,

Disciples of Christ, United Brethren and the Philippine Methodist Church merged to form the United Church of Christ in the Philippines [UCCP].)

The American Baptist Missionary Union and the Christian and Missionary Alliance arrived in the Philippines at about the same time, the former concentrating on the islands of Negros and Panay, while the latter began operations in Mindanao. They were followed after a year by the United Brethren and the Disciples of Christ, who confined most of their work to the northern part of Luzon, while maintaining ties in other parts of the same island. The Congregationalists arrived as early as 1902 but were understaffed for several years; they had difficulty expanding their work until after the arrival of the famous missionary Frank Laubach,[8] who pioneered adult literacy work in the Philippines and worldwide. Six years later, in 1908, the Seventh Day Adventists established their mission under the watchful and often unwelcoming eyes of missionaries of the other churches.

Though not without struggles and difficulties, Philippine Protestant efforts prospered during the first twenty-five years. With the faithful support of their mother churches in the U.S. and Europe, denominational memberships increased from year to year, giving birth to new local congregations both in the cities and in the far-flung areas of the country. The work was facilitated by the fact that many of the new colonial administrators, businesspeople and school teachers were Protestants.

"Foreign mission," as we noted earlier, was not simply confined to organizing new congregations or to personal witness. Given the urgency of the times, missionaries extended welfare assistance in the form of such basic services as hospitals, clinics, schools and orphanages. In practically no time at all, such facilities spread to various parts of the country, serving not only recognized members of Protestant churches but the general public as well. A number of them have survived to this day, and some have expanded and modernized their services and facilities. It is apparent that these

ministries have contributed immensely to the social
and economic development of certain towns and cities
across the country.

But it cannot be denied that however important the
foreign missionaries' role might have been in proclaim-
ing the gospel and expanding Christian tradition to
non-Christian peoples, they also had the important role
across the Asian region of advancing and representing
the interests of their mother country. Considered to
be an articulate breed of intellectuals, missionaries had
plenty of influence in shaping public opinion on
questions affecting Philippine-American relations and
in determining policies related to their country's allies.
They were certainly among those who helped guide
the American public's perceptions regarding Philippine
society and culture and what their country needed to
do to help the Filipinos "develop" themselves.

It could be said that the missionaries were of great
help in reorienting Filipinos to their new colonial
situation. They did not, however, encourage people to
ask critical questions regarding their political possibilities as a nation. Had the missionaries encouraged a
truly candid and critical interpretation of Philippine-
American relations and the issues and problems these
posed,* the scope and content of evangelical witness
in the Philippines would have taken a different turn,
theologically and otherwise. This is rather ironic,
considering that a substantial number of Filipinos
became Protestants precisely because of their negative
reaction to the colonial Catholic church.

Knowing that the experience of oppression and abuse
under the Spanish friars was still fresh in the memory
of the Filipino people, Protestant missionaries often
directed their doctrinal polemics against the Roman
Catholic Church, explicitly claiming for themselves a
more enlightened faith. Seeing the Catholic Church as
an archrival in Christian crusade, they concentrated
heavily on the conversion of Catholics to Protestantism,

---

* Editors' note: Self-determination was indeed an issue, however, as
reflected in the Protestant Chronology (page 160). Some significant church
controversies and divisions occurred because of this.

virtually making numerical growth in membership the avowed task of Christian mission.

Needless to say, this had a profoundly limiting effect on Filipinos' socio-political awareness. Preoccupied with religious doctrine, the Filipino mind was drawn away from the urgency of the historical situation, namely, the ongoing Filipino resistance to outside rule (which had become American rule) and the people's yearning for genuine national independence. From the very beginning, the Protestantism inherited by the Filipino people was unwilling to courageously address the nagging questions of the nation's political life. It is no wonder that we have not, to this day, gone far enough in influencing our own history's movement toward a truly liberating course.

Strides toward self-reliance, autonomy and faithfulness

The quick proliferation of mission groups during the first few years of U.S. rule brought problems of jurisdictional overlapping, segregation and cases of proselytism among Protestants. This was given due attention by the concerned missionaries, resulting in the formation of what they called the "Evangelical Union." As described by Peter Gowing, this was:

> 1) a comity arrangement dividing the country among the various missions with a view to avoiding overlapping, competition and duplication of work; and
> 2) the assumption of a common name for all the Protestant congregations—The Evangelical Church—with the denominational name being added in parentheses....[9]

The growing evangelical community was not, however, content with the drive for unity among Protestants, a sentiment which became associated with the expression of the desire for truly self-governing, autonomous churches. This led to the gradual reduction of missionary involvement in the leadership of the evangelical movement and, later, to missionaries' secession of control. Though this latter purpose was not entirely achieved, consolidation and nationalization of Christian mission programs were partially accomplished in the previously mentioned historic merger of closely allied churches and denominations to form the United Church of Christ in the Philippines.

The move toward unity and self-government was also concretely demonstrated in the formation of the Philippine Federation of Evangelical Churches, which later evolved into what is known today as the National Council of Churches in the Philippines (NCCP). Starting with at least seven denominational members and other church-related entities, the council has, over the years, welcomed more Christian bodies, mostly from mainstream Protestant groups.

It is with the emergence of the ecumenical movement that we in the Philippines can best illustrate how Protestant institutions today express their faithfulness in mission and ministry. Through the ecumenical movement, churches have become more effective vehicles for interpreting and responding to the country's socio-political challenges. This fact marks a radical departure from old patterns of religious witness and service. Under the militarized government of Ferdinand Marcos, for instance, the NCCP's official statements and prophetic pronouncements were given serious attention by the ruling powers, although in most cases the latter interpreted them as unseemly for religious bodies to make. A church pastor once remarked that matters dealing with socio-political problems had brought Protestants and Catholics closer together than at any other time in the country's religious history.

Ecumenical cooperation in the Philippines today has gone beyond the old confines of Protestant sectarian circles, and more and more common ventures in mission and Christian engagement are being inaugurated between groups that used to be "doctrinal enemies." Interestingly, through ecumenical cooperation, faithfulness to mission has become a more truly open possibility for both Protestants and Catholics.

Of course, expressions of Christian faithfulness in Protestant circles are not simply limited to what we see through the NCCP. In education, for example, the Association of Christian Schools and Colleges, a Protestant initiative organized many years ago, is committed to assisting individual Protestant schools all over the country on many levels of need, including curriculum improvement and faculty development. While many of the schools in the association are presently confronted with various crises, having been affected directly or indirectly by the nation's political and economic setbacks during the Marcos years, their leaders continue to be in good spirits, doing what they can to manage their respective situations.

The Philippine Bible Society is another major area of cooperation, not only among Filipino evangelicals but involving Roman Catholics as well. Through the years the society has translated the Bible or portions of the Bible into most Philippine languages and dialects, has continued to update many of these translations, and has distributed thousands of Bibles to a great number of people, institutions and churches all over the country. This helps greatly in supporting mission work among those who at least understand the "languages of the cities," and among those who have not attained the education necessary to be conversant in the colonial language.

Campus ministries are widely undertaken, both ecumenically and through local church initiatives. A typical example of the former is the University of the Philippines Protestant Ministry. Though procedurally under the auspices of the NCCP, the university ministry has attained self-sufficiency because of the abiding and generous support of the local congregation that came into existence several years after the student ministry began. Over the years, this ministry has become a leading partner in the ecumenical movement, not only in the area of student work, but also by assisting small local churches and their workers. The ministry has

recently established a foundation that helps send
students to theological seminaries. Since it operates
under no particular denomination, the ministry
welcomes into its membership all people regardless of
religious affiliation or political persuasion.

Recent additions to Protestant ecumenical work are
such organizations as the Ecumenical Center for
Development (ECD) and the Institute of Religion and
Culture (IRC), both of which have demonstrated a great
sense of solidarity with various groups in Philippine
society that have been struggling against repression
since the early years of the Marcos regime. ECD is
mainly concerned with the socio-economic uplifting of
poor and neglected communities. Its aim is to help
people discover alternative development strategies and
to raise their socio-political consciousness towards
greater participation in restoring popular democratic
principles. IRC, on the other hand, helps churchpeople
and other groups and communities explore possible
cultural sources for change in society. It initiates
dialogue among people of various professions and holds
forums with labor unions, women's groups, the urban
poor and the like, offering them alternative ways of
being heard.

Organizations of a similar nature are also found in
the islands of Visayas and Mindanao. Though they
certainly have different emphases, they are united in
the principle of solidarity with the poor and powerless
in society.

Much more could be said of the multifarious forms
of non-Catholic belief and organization in the
Philippines (see Appendix: Outline of Christian
Churches in the Philippines). Each one has its unique
character and nature of religious practice. More than
one book would be needed to take serious account
of their stories. Certainly, these forms are important,
each doing its part in appealing to people's hearts.

On the whole, Philippine Protestantism has made
a significant contribution to the growth of the nation.
While it remains a small religious community compared
to the Roman Catholic Church, it is influential, and

we must note the growing base of the ecumenical movement. The challenges of recent history have undoubtedly served to stimulate and educate both its leadership and its constituencies. Surely, many more challenges and tests of faith lie ahead.

NOTES

1. Philippine Protestants claim the term "evangelical," as have most Protestant missionaries to the Philippines, stressing the proclamation of the gospel and the creation of new local churches.
2. The notion of "manifest destiny" is well articulated in Gerard H. Anderson, "Providence and Politics behind Protestant Missionary Beginnings in the Philippines," in his edited work *Studies in Philippine Church History* (Ithaca and London: Cornell University Press, 1969), pp. 279-300. This article is invaluable for those interested in Protestant involvement in the early debate about whether or not the United States should colonize the Philippines. It carries some facinating quotations from primary sources.
3. Recent works of Philippine historians have disputed the claim that Commodore Dewey indeed defeated Spain in a naval battle in Manila Bay (see footnote, page 14). For some detailed accounts, see Renato Constantino, *The Philippines: A Past Revisited*, Vol. I (Quezon City, Philippines: Renato Constantino, 1975); Stuart Creighton Miller, *Benevolent Assimilation* (New Haven: Yale Univ. Press, 1982), p. 43; and Luzviminda Francisco, "The Philippines, End of an Illusion," *Bulletin of Concerned Asian Scholars*, (London, 1973).
4. Anderson, *op. cit.*, p. 289.
5. Ibid., p. 282.
6. Constantino, Ibid., p. 247.
7. For a resourceful documentation of this see Kenton J. Clymer, *Protestant Missionaries in the Philippines, 1898-1916* (Urbana and Chicago: University of Illinois Press, 1986), pp. 1-8.
8. Richard L. Deats, *Nationalism and Christianity in the Philippines* (Dallas: Southern Methodist University Press, 1967), pp. 100-101.
9. Peter G. Gowing, *Islands Under the Cross* (Manila: National Council of Churches in the Philippines, 1967), p. 127.

Editors' Note

Living in a world of bitterly competing ideologies, faced with the particular tension between the major economic systems of capitalism and communism, people of faith must press hard amid the noise to raise deep ethical questions about "development."

What, for Christians striving to live in light of the Bible and in continuing encounter with the living, caring Christ, is authentic human development? What kind of development will affirm and nurture the integrity of God's image in us and in all creation?

Strangely enough, both communism and capitalism are powerfully secular systems. Both are unabashedly materialistic and both are on the defensive, neither displaying the power to win over the people of a world desperately searching for workable solutions to seemingly unending economic and political problems.

Nationalistic peoples' movements from the "underside of history," which are largely organized movements of poor people struggling for selfhood, liberation and justice, show great strength and determination as they seek not only to throw off domination, but also to find new answers appropriate to their situations.

This is especially true in the Philippines. Who would question that Filipinos are justified in insisting that there has to be a better way for ordering their economic and political development?

All systems and movements are under the judgment of God. In the Philippines, however, it is capitalism that is being very harshly judged. Edna Orteza's moving chapter puts a human face on poverty in the Philippines and helps us to see the deep historical roots of mal-development. She shows us why the removal of a dictator and a sense of "getting things moving again" are not enough. While she does not attempt to prescribe answers, Orteza's vignettes of the lives of ordinary Filipinos illustrate people's capacity for struggle, which is both a gift from God and a sign of hope.

THE ELUSIVE QUEST FOR DEVELOPMENT

Edna J. Orteza

How do we tell our story? Do we speak in anger? With shame and remorse? Or with courage and hope? How would you understand our longing to share a different story and break away from the shackles of our perverse history?

Is it possible to speak a common language? Though we have come to learn English, our words evoke different meanings, and we have diverse memories of our varying experiences.

You see, somewhere in our colonial past, our history began to be intertwined with yours. But somehow this linking also signaled the great divide. Privilege, power, progress and development marked the high points of your own history. Ours continued on towards poverty, dependency, powerlessness and underdevelopment.

So, how do we attempt a common understanding? How do we forge a unity so that together we can close the gaps?

In order to trace the roots of our inequality, we may have to break imposed lines, touch painful points, clarify elements of misunderstanding and mistrust. We will need to remember children, women and men who, through no fault of their own, have become victims of injustice arising from historical economic relation-

Edna J. Orteza is the director of the Department of Christian Education of the United Church of Christ in the Philippines. She was formerly director of the Center for Mindanao Missions of Cagayan de Oro City.

ships and conditions. Some of them I have known personally:

Lita, a mother of six, who must bear the burden of keeping her family alive by doing other people's laundry because her husband could not find work in the city, where farming skills have no place. How many times and in how many destructive ways has she attempted to escape the quagmire of her poverty?

Eladio, a father of seven, who, to escape poverty in Leyte, migrated to the south with his peasant family and who must suffer the pain of seeing his children dying one after another of malnutrition and disease.

Placido, a farmer who must watch his plants destroyed, his chickens killed, his house demolished and his family driven out to give way to a transnational corporation expansion program.

Eloy, just a boy, crying in his anger, holding on to his dog—his friend and companion in lonely and hungry days—dead in his arms, shot by soldiers for barking at them during a counter-insurgency campaign.

These are ordinary people with ordinary dreams who have not heard of genetic engineering or satellite stations and rocketships that can take people to the moon. The moon of their dreams is a quiet evening where no dogs howl in fear because strange people have come in the night to change the course of their lives. These are people who dream to be themselves, to sing lullabys to their sleeping children, and to be able to greet each new morning with certainty and hope.

What does it mean to be poor?

It means gnawing pain in the stomach after a day without meals. It means eating a boiled banana and saving the peel for the night. It means back-breaking labor to bring home a kilo of rice. It means watching your children die because you could not feed them enough.

Being poor means not being able to send your children to school because they, too, have to work—exposed to the elements, weeding, planting, harvesting, tapping rubber trees or peddling cigarettes and flowers in dangerous places and at busy intersections of city streets. It means growing up in ignorance in order to survive.

Being poor means living daily with the threat of eviction, of waking up one morning to find your house being bulldozed, the walls which, together, your family has painfully put up, breaking into pieces. And then you realize you have nowhere to go.

Being poor also means the humiliation and shame of begging the loan shark to give you more time to settle your account even if you know it is impossible. It is anguish at the realization that you are left without choices, so that for a few pesos you would sell your right to vote.

Poverty alienates. It drives people to make impossible choices. It means women selling their bodies to support starving families; parents selling the "favors" of their children to moneyed, fair-skinned pedophiles,* all for the opportunity to start a small business; mothers leaving their own children to care for other mothers' babies, often abroad, to earn a few dollars; fathers enduring loneliness in the Middle East to send their children to school; young people going into drugs to escape their daily realities.

Why are we poor? Why do some people have to suffer pain and humiliation for a meal? Why do some people have money to make other people work for them? Why do some people have the power and influence to decide other people's future?

---

* Those having a sexual attraction to children.

And here I am, uncomfortably contemplating the awkward way Nena and her mother are cleaning the dust-ridden glass panes of the windows of my house. Escaping poverty and armed conflict in their barrio, they have come to clean my windows, prepare our meals, do our laundry, care for my grandchildren. They brought nothing and left nothing in their empty shack, the other children given away so that they, too, could live.

I grew up believing that poverty was a consequence of God's will, that it was no cause for guilt, that we could eat, go to school, have other people work for us because God had made it so. But I grew up, and the innocent questions of poverty ultimately became issues of justice and development.

This consciousness, however, did not bring much change in the lives of people I have known. So they are still with me, haunting every moral fiber, awaiting transformation.

I was to realize that historically, poverty is rooted in the social relations spawned by the domination of the strong over the weak and the powerless.

Lita, Eladio, Placido, Eloy, and Nena and her mother are victims of forces and circumstances beyond their control. They are victims of a global economic system that gives high priority to increased productivity, economic growth, scientific innovation, new technology, nuclearization and military superiority. It is an economic and political order that enslaves and impoverishes some so that others may be richer and more powerful.

It seems that when some people are becoming richer and more powerful, this is called "development."

For the poor, who have neither memory nor experience of such a concept, development remains an elusive dream.

The Philippines, said to be a "developing" country, provides no visible indication of a growing capacity to increase the well-being of its ordinary people. The dynamics of the socio-economic, political and cultural processes in present society certainly are not evidence of such a trend in the near future. Instead, the country and its people are sinking deeper into poverty.

There are milllions of Eladios and Nenas in my country, living in imposed poverty, degraded by hunger and malnutrition, disease and ignorance resulting from historically rooted social relationships in which the concentration of wealth and power in the hands of a few has caused the poverty and marginalization of many.

> Claveria, Misamis Oriental [north Mindanao], became the site of military operations from February to April 1986. Spearheaded by the Scout Rangers, paramilitary and fanatic groups, and backed up by helicopter gunships, the operations rendered sixteen people dead. They were dumped in a common pit. One woman was reported raped before she was mutilated and murdered.
>
> Part of the counter-insurgency program of the government, the military operation in Claveria had forced the evacuation of two thousand people. Due to cramped, unsanitary conditions at the evacuation centers, nine children had died of dysentery and pneumonia. The evacuees reported that soldiers and fanatics had strafed villages, looted and burned eighty-five houses to the ground.*

So, to survive, the people leave the countryside and try the cities. They take risks, selling their few possessions, perhaps their only *carabao* (water buffalo) or their only piece of land.

But opportunities are rare, and they become unemployment statistics on the charts. They live in any unoccupied space, building shanties out of scrap materials salvaged from the wastes of the affluent. To survive, they scavange, beg, sell lottery tickets, do odd jobs. They striptease and dance to the music of Madonna and Boy George, providing "color" for American sailors in noisy Olongapo.

---

* From the Task Force Detainees Philippines' publication, *Mindanao Report.*

The luckier ones are employed in factories, ports, marketplaces or offices to do menial jobs. Without experience or skills and left without choices, they are again subjected to exploitative conditions in their areas of work.

Many skilled Filipinos leave the country to work overseas as entertainers, domestic helpers, chambermaids, hospital aides, construction workers, seamen, technical and medical professionals. Reduced to the level of commodity, bought and sold in the capitalist marketplace at prices fixed by those who control it, they lose much of their dignity and self-respect.

> Four Filipina domestic workers in Kuwait will face imprisonment immediately after giving birth to their babies, who were conceived after their employers sexually abused them.
>
> Kuwaiti laws specify that mothers must produce marriage certificates to claim their babies and avoid the death-by-stoning penalty for immorality.
>
> This has prompted the former minister of Foreign Affairs to write the Philippine Embassy in Kuwait to look into the case.*

Indeed, why should the Philippines, a country so rich in natural resources and vast mineral reserves, be so poor? Why should the people who work the land be the first to go hungry and become afflicted with severe conditions of poverty? Why should people become refugees in strange lands just because they are poor?

The historical roots of underdevelopment in the Philippines

Our ancestors were not exactly poor. They lived in small, scattered ethnic communities and subsisted on fishing, hunting and food gathering. No one had a monopoly on the land and the resources derived from

---

* News from *KAIBIGAN*, a cause-oriented organization concerned with the plight of Filipino migrant workers. After vigorous protests by Philippine officials, the workers were released and returned to the Philippines.

it were shared by all. Communities were organized into *barangays* and headed by *datus*. The Moro people in the south had the highest socio-political formation, with Islam as a dominant feature in their religious and social life.

By colonial standards their economy may have seemed primitive and backward, but it was relatively self-sufficient. It did not allow sharp class divisions that would thrive on the exploitation of the weak. The economy also showed manifestations of a slow but well-founded growth. In fact, at the point of conquest, extensive areas of land had already been cultivated. The people had domesticated animals, were weaving their own clothes, and were manufacturing metal tools and ornaments that they later traded with neighboring countries.

The essence of the communal life arising from this indigenous political economy was radically disrupted with the arrival of the Spaniards in the sixteenth century. Immediately, social relations changed. Land became a point of contention. Land was appropriated by Spanish officials, soldiers, settlers and friars. Land was also awarded to local chieftains, who became the principal collaborators in the subjugation of the people.

Land no longer belonged to the people. On the contrary, they had became captive farmworkers, forced to produce not for themselves but for the new feudal lords. Landless and burdened with taxes, they were driven into lifelong indebtedness that often spanned three generations. Granddaughters enslaved themselves in the masters' homes to pay for debts incurred before they were born.

Through this period of feudalism, that lasted throughout the Industrial Revolution and the rise of capitalism in Europe, the Philippine economy was increasingly drawn into the world market. As the Spaniards brought in foreign investments, new technology, scientific agriculture, and infrastructures to boost large-scale production of consumption goods and increase profits for the landed entrepreneurs, the people were reduced to a mere element of production. They became more and more alienated from the land and this alienation found refuge in religion. The church became the center of people's devotion, and the friars, assuming greater power, instilled a new set of values that would dominate Filipino consciousness for centuries. Rebellion against authorities was seen as rebellion against God and deserving of eternal damnation. Passivity, docility, sacrifice and human suffering were regarded as virtues; people would be given their final reward in heaven. Rigorous catechism in schools reinforced such cultural impositions.

Then, in 1898, the Americans came.

Under U.S. rule, the Free Trade Policy was imposed. It allowed all American goods to enter the Philippines tax free and in unlimited quantities. In turn, the Philippines was to export its raw materials to the United States. But the Philippines, basically agrarian and feudal, could in no way be in an equal relationship with the U.S. In fact, through the decades of American rule, the U.S. economy would thrive on the feudal structure. The Philippine economy would become even more vulnerable through a series of treaties, acts, agreements and laws. Essentially, the Philippines was made subservient to U.S. policies.[1]

Public education also helped to broaden American influence. With American textbooks, American curricula and American teachers, and with English as the medium of instruction, the Americanization of the "little brown brother" (a term used regularly in that era by American leaders) began.[2]

The American myth became an obsession: America is the land of opportunity; in America, all are equal; American products are superior; Americans came to provide Filipinos democracy, education and training in self-government so that they could eventually be independent; America is the great benefactor. The conquerors became heroes.[3]

This colonial consciousness made free trade seem indispensable to economic growth and increased the general feeling of dependence on the United States. Landlords, conveniently placed in government positions, became increasingly reluctant to exchange their lucrative positions for the uncertainties of freedom. In spite of growing anti-American sentiment among ordinary Filipinos, the educated, landed, powerful elite became the new colonizers' most reliable allies.

American domination of the Philippines continued, only briefly interrupted by three years of Japanese Occupation (1942-1945). Their country left ravaged by the war, Filipinos came to depend increasingly upon the U.S. The general feeling, in fact, was one of gratitude and relief that the Americans had not actually left. Filipinos generally did not see any conflict between the interests of the "conqueror" and the "conquered."

The near half-century of American rule had so thoroughly restructured Philippine economy, politics and culture that even after "independence" in 1946, the new republic remained nearly totally subservient to American policies. Filipinos had become politically independent without the liberation of their consciousness to assert that independence.

The Bell Trade Act and the Parity Amendment further assured the Americans of continuing free trade relations with the Philippines.[4] The Philippines signed a Military Bases Agreement with the United States, which gave the U.S. twenty-three base sites for ninety-nine years, renewable on expiration.[5] It also provided American military officials exclusive jurisdiction over all American personnel. Over the years, this would provoke angry protests from Filipinos who resented the fact that American soldiers who had shot or abused Filipinos could not be tried in Philippine courts, but were conveniently transferred to U.S. military bases outside of the Philippines.

In exchange for these special agreements, the U.S. government sent aid in the form of war reparations payments to enable the country to reconstruct its economy. However, the slow rehabilitation of traditional export industries and the increased demand for imported goods made trade relations more favorable to the U.S. Hardly able to fill our trade quotas, we were flooded with finished products from the U.S.;

always buying more and selling less, our economy plunged into crisis after crisis.

Within three years after the end of the war our country was on the verge of upheaval: economic reconstruction was slow; production was slow; unemployment was widespread; crime was rampant; landlords had set up private armies; peasants and workers were restive. The Communist-led Hukbong Mapagpalaya ng Bayan (Huks), the People's Liberation Army, was gaining widespread support and by 1950 was already in the outskirts of Manila.[6] This rebellion, however, was eventually contained by the military successes of President Magsaysay with the political and military support of the United States.

Programs for reform were launched and a military/police framework was developed that would make severe repression possible. Feudal estates were broken up, ostensibly for distribution to the peasants. In essence, however, "reform" meant the replacement of backward farm practices by scientific methods, and the number of landless families actually increased. The entry of big business was given impetus with the drive for increased productivity and new technology.

The process we call neo-colonialism had begun.

Capitalist models in an agrarian economy

This is not to say that no attempts have been made to alleviate human suffering. Rather, it is to assert that government efforts have tended to increase economic dependency, indebtedness, cultural domination and internal conflict.

The Philippines has pursued economic development strategies that are corollary to the interests of big business, in effect preserving and aggravating dependency relationships in the economy. The orientation of the economy almost totally around exports subjects the country's resources to the utilization and allocation priorities of big business. We cannot escape the fact that this is characterized by the continuing extraction and depletion of natural, mineral and marine resources;

by the development of infrastructures to facilitate this extraction; by further foreign investment; by the strengthening of foreign-controlled technology; and by increased borrowing from foreigners. While the country appears to be integrating itself more fully into the international economic order, in reality it remains far out on the periphery, deeper and deeper into dependency and debt, continuing to produce raw materials so that a few can reap profits.

Let us look at some of these strategies.

The Green Revolution

One such strategy was the "Green Revolution," based on the inventions of U.S. geneticists. Intended to increase rice production, the Green Revolution gained popularity in the sixties, mainly through the International Rice Research Institute (IRRI), a research center dedicated to the discovery and distribution of high-yielding varieties of rice for all of Asia.

There is high financing involved in the Green Revolution. The IRRI, for instance, is financed by the Rockefeller and Ford Foundations and by a funding consortium called the Consultative Group on International Agricultural Research (CGIAR). The consortium was established in 1971 in New York under the auspices of the World Bank (WB), the United Nations Development Program (UNDP) and the Food and Agriculture Organization (FAO) of the United Nations.[7]

The Philippine government responded enthusiastically to the Green Revolution program and launched wide-scale promotion of its merits. When the World Bank, the United States' Agency for International Development (US AID), and the Asian Development Bank (ADB) insisted on the intensification of rice production as a condition for the granting of much-desired loans, the Philippine government complied by increasing rice output within a limited area of land so that more land could be appropriated for export crops, which was the real interest of the agribusiness capitalists.

How was rice output increased? The government induced the production of up to three crops a year under the "Masagana 99" campaign program, so-called because it attempted to produce ninety-nine cavans (large jute sacks) per hectare (2.45 acres). This caused radical changes in agronomic practices. It required inputs far beyond the financial capabilities of most farmers in terms of fertilizers, herbicides, insecticides and other chemicals. The kind of fertilizer used required good irrigation control in order to be effective. Moreover, the "miracle rice" varieties matured early. Since more crops were planted each year, the period of time between crops became very short and the land had little time for recovery. So "miracle rice" varieties required miracles in order to yield the expected results!

Ordinary farmers were not generally able to cope with the Green Revolution. The high cost of production and the low prices set for the produce had devastating effects. Not uncommonly, when land was used as collateral for loans it was lost to its lenders. The farmers became poorer, hungrier and more deeply in debt.

Agricultural loans

Large-scale loans were another economic strategy, and as pointed out earlier, these went hand-in-hand with the Green Revolution. To facilitate the wide-scale production of "miracle rice" varieties, the government made agricultural loans readily available to farmers. But, again, the loan schemes proved to be favorable mainly to the "owners" of the money, those with capital. They were insured, and couldn't lose!

Banks accompanied credit schemes with much supervision and control, especially in the case of farmers who were considered incapable of managing farm operations. In effect, banks decided what crops would be grown, how and when to plant, what fertilizers to use, what pesticides to buy, when to sell, to whom, and for how much. If not released in the form of things such as fertilizers, seeds, insecticides, etc., the loan itself was granted in small amounts, since "farmers did not know how to handle money."

The loan schemes left farmers with few choices. After their produce was appropriated for previous debts, they did not have savings for both buying rice to eat and producing their next crop. With their family subsistence needs always unfulfilled, farmers had traditionally tended to divert portions of loans to buy food for their families—one reason why they were frustrated when loans came in the form of fertilizers and pesticides. As should have been expected, loans were often not fully repaid, or not repaid at all.

It is revealing that bank policies were different for large borrowers. Considered to be of good social, economic and political standing ("good risks"), they were the preferred clients, who for mere speculation could obtain long-term loans. They also diverted loans, and did so for such non-productive ventures as real estate speculation and travel abroad, as well as to gain access to political power.

The Green Revolution and the accompanying agricultural loan programs provide an example of how hunger and poverty can become the pretext for more investment without a consideration of the social, political and ecological context in which farmers relate to the land. Their affinity to the land, their first-hand knowledge of the possibilities of the soil and climate, as well as their special attachment to the plants and all other forms of life involved are usually ignored. Instead, outsiders, often foreigners, whose farming skills are limited to research findings on rice seeds, chemicals and farm machinery and whose skill in economics is limited to theory and macro-indicators, are allowed to dominate the land and become its main beneficiaries.

With agricultural loans the "planners" tied loan schemes (for generations used against farmers) to national economic strategies, forcing the farmers into a humiliating state of dependency on a national scale.

When those who have been farming all their lives lose the possibility for making decisions over the land, their alienation becomes absolute. They are pushed out, forced to search for unusual solutions.

Agribusiness corporations

At the same time as the so-called Green Revolution, national agricultural priorities shifted from the production of food crops to the production of commercial crops for export. Ernest Feder calls it "The Other Green Revolution."[8] This shift was widely promoted to boost big-time farming and the processing and trading of export and luxury foods, animal feeds and industrial raw materials. It was in reality an outright government endorsement of the expansion of transnational agribusiness corporations' domination of the Philippine economy.

Because of its vast agricultural and forest land and mining and marine resources, Mindanao became the main target for transnational corporations' (TNCs') expansion programs in the country. During the 1970s, agribusiness ventures exploited huge tracts of land in Mindanao that had previously been occupied by countless small farm families.

Philippine law provides that corporate landholdings be limited to 1,024 hectares. TNCs, however, have been able to make claims on vast tracts of land for agribusiness. The California Packing Corporation, for example, established a Philippine subsidiary called the Philippine Packing Corporation, which leased 16,000 hectares of land in Mindanao from the government.[9]

How do the corporations get around the law? They circumvent it through local capitalists, government officials or through the National Development Corporation. These groups have been only too willing to make land acquisitions for foreign investors because of the benefits they get through their association with them.

With the expansion of the TNCs, land became increasingly concentrated in the hands of a foreign-controlled elite. All aspects of the Philippine economy are now under TNC influence or control, including the production and processing of raw materials and the distribution and consumption of finished products.

The TNCs' profit orientation has aggravated the impoverished condition of people in the rural areas. Local people have gradually been dispossessed of their land and virtually enslaved on the new plantations. And plantations employ only some of the local people who need jobs, because owners prefer capital-intensive technology. STANFILCO, for example, the banana growing subsidiary of the Dole Corporation, employs only one worker per thirteen hectares of land.[10]

The agricultural workers suffer from exploitative conditions on the plantations:

> On the rubber plantations, mothers and children have to assist the fathers, for the wages of one, in order to meet the quota for the day.
>
> On banana plantations, eighty percent of the workers work in the fields—weeding, planting, spraying pesticides, putting fertilizers on the soil, pruning. There are baggers who wrap bananas in newspapers and in plastic bags to protect the fruit from the sun and from pests. There are those who check which fruits are ready for harvest and which ones are rejects. There are those who harvest the fruits and must carry thirty to forty kilos of banana bundles. The field workers are daily exposed either to sun or rain. They are without shelter, and sometimes have only banana leaves to protect them from heavy rains. They also suffer diseases resulting from exposure to chemicals and from the indiscriminate use of fertilizers and pesticides.

Low wages, high production quotas, forced overtime, inadequate protection from health and production hazards, poor medical services and miserable housing conditions are the most common problems and complaints of plantation workers.

In Negros, sugar workers receive only 26.18 pesos ($1.39) as a daily wage—with no overtime pay and no social security. They usually work for 10 months each year. Other members of the family work to augment the income, including 8- to 9-year-old children who are paid only 2 to 3 pesos (10 to 15 cents) per day.*

After the slump in the sugar market (mid-1980s), two-thirds of the sugar workers were rendered unemployed. Because nearly the whole island was planted with sugar cane, other staple foods were scarce and therefore expensive. Even the sugar they produced was not available to them, and if it was, they did not have any money to buy it.

Without benefits and without security of tenure, plantation workers also have to contend with harassment by plantation security guards and the military when they make the slightest show of resistance.

"They do not care about us, as long as we are able to work in the plantation each day...."

"We are like prisoners here. Our life revolves around these bananas. Day in and day out, we see nothing but bananas."

"What future will our children have in this situation?"

Infrastructures

All roads lead to big business.

The strategy for agricultural development features massive infrastructure projects: the construction of ports, roads, bridges and highways that provide ease and accessibility in the transport of raw materials into the international market.

These projects provide a semblance of modernization in the countryside. Electric posts lining the highways in Mindanao, for instance, give the impression that all houses must have electricity. On the contrary, even

---

* As of December 1987, the nominal daily wage (national average) for a plantation worker was $2.92. Sugar workers are often far below the national average, however, and many workers are either "informal" or non-regular workers, or contract workers, who receive significantly less than the legal minimum wage.

houses along the highways do not have such easy access: expensive wires, bulbs and switches are a low priority for most families, who are struggling to find enough to eat.

These infrastructures mainly benefit the economic interests of big business. Rough roads would simply not do for fruits, food crops and marine resources, which are perishable and therefore require immediate transport.

Hinatuan and Lianga Bay in Surigao del Sur are rich in water resources, especially prawns and crabs. Interested in setting up a "fish quarry" where these could be cultured, Japanese investors have funded the construction of the international port of nearby Butuan City. Ports are also needed to facilitate the movement of international ships to load bananas, coconut products, pineapple, coffee and timber, as well as to unload the related machinery and supplies from other countries.

Airports provide travel convenience for investors and business executives. Hotels, casinos and beach resorts likewise provide for the leisure required after profitable business transactions.

The construction of these infrastructures is itself a big enterprise that allows the accumulation of greater profits for the investors and lending institutions that provide the funds for capital-intensive projects.

Again, the ordinary people do not benefit from this development strategy. Access to infrastructures requires money. Comfort and convenience have to be paid for!

And the people have paid dearly. The construction of dams—the Chico Dam, the Ambuklao Dam or the Pulangi River Basin Project—have caused the dislocation of thousands of families. These dams have, in fact, caused the flooding of whole communities, mostly the village sites of Tribal Filipinos. This has prompted a series of protests in which many Tribal Filipinos have died.

Export processing zones

Export Processing Zones (EPZs) are part of the comprehensive economic development strategy of the Philippine government. These are designed to enhance industrialization by providing more jobs, by creating satellite industrial centers in the rural areas, and by diversifying export production. This strategy implies that the Philippines is involved not only in production but also in the processing of raw materials in a more systematic and modern way.

The Bataan Export Processing Zone (BEPZ) is the biggest EPZ. It occupies an isolated, secure area of 1,209 hectares, complete with facilities for loading and unloading, storing and shipping exports and imports without customs duties. Construction of the BEPZ caused the dislocation of 841 families in two barrios. Most of them now live in a squalid squatter community outside of the zone.

There are some fifty corporations operating in the zone, mostly controlled by Japanese investors and Filipino capitalists and joint ventures, among them the Ford Philippines Stamping Plant, Soltron Electronics, Lotus Export Specialists, Ricoh Watch, Hitachi and AMCO Jeans. Consistent with the favorable conditions provided these TNCs, they enjoy tax incentives, are assured of cheap labor and are protected from labor disputes.

The BEPZ employs 28 thousand workers, most of whom live in overcrowded dormitories outside the zone. The majority are women—young, single, inexperienced, unskilled and vulnerable to exploitative practices within the factories.

> Overtime work is often imposed on the workers, who lose their jobs if they refuse. Company restrictions prevent workers from leaving work even when they are sick. Overtime pay is 1.60 pesos (8 cents) per hour. The daily average wage is 28 pesos ($1.40), but most workers take home only 10 pesos (50 cents) after deductions.

The women workers work long, monotonous hours, straining their eyes through microscopes, putting together minute parts of watches or microchips, sewing thousands of sleeves of Barbie Doll clothes. They are hired for their youth (being fifteen to twenty years old) and for the dexterity of their fingers to do delicate jobs.

The nuclear power plant

The construction of the Bataan Nuclear Power Plant (BNPP) was for a long time a major source of controversy in the Philippines, given the context of widespread poverty. This grandiose scheme helped to bring into perspective the extent of corruption during the Marcos regime.

The project should be seen in the context of export-oriented industrialization. The BNPP was part of the electrification program required by WB/US AID and the U.S. Export-Import Bank to make electricity available to industry and to all by 1990.[11]

The BNPP was contracted by the National Power Corporation from Westinghouse, without public bidding, originally for a price of $500 million, which had escalated to $1.9 billion by 1976,[12] and with a currently estimated cost of $2 billion. It was reported that a relative of former president Marcos received a multi-million dollar fee from Westinghouse during the negotiations. The same relative was also the sub-contractor and the owner of insurance companies that received generous government contracts during the construction of the plant.

Beyond the corruption issue were major unresolved safety problems brought up by safety engineers and anti-nuclear activists. Controversy delayed construction: the site was particularly vulnerable to earthquakes; that particular Westinghouse design had been shown to pose hazards to health and safety; safeguards were grossly insufficient; the disposal of nuclear waste was inadequately provided for. The hazards to human life intrinsic to this nuclear project are incalculable.

But the United States State Department has defended the reactor, giving as its reason that:

> ...an adequate and growing supply of electric power is particularly essential for developing countries. Agriculture, manufacturing, schools and hospitals as well as every other sector of the economy and all levels of society depend on electric power and there can be no significant development without it.[13]

The nuclear reactor was supposed to lessen the country's dependence on foreign sources of energy by reducing consumption of imported oil. On the contrary, it would place the country in total dependence upon Westinghouse and the U.S. Government for uranium fuel, maintenance, spare parts and the disposal of radioactive wastes. Designed to operate for only thirty years (an economic life limited by the usual radioactive contamination), it was a very costly way to lessen dependence! The reality of this project is that the cost of electricity and of basic commodities and taxes will increase and the people will be further burdened.

There are energy alternatives in the Philippines that can actually be developed, including geothermal, hydroelectric, coal and non-conventional sources which, according to statistics, would provide 54 percent of total energy requirements in 1995 and would utilize only 36 percent of total power development expenditures. In contrast, the BNPP, if operated, will have only a 3 to 4 percent share in the provision of total energy requirements but will itself have required 43 percent of the total power development cost.[14]

The generation of a limited amount of energy at a cost of billions of dollars is a crime, especially when over seven million Filipinos, many of whom are malnourished, live within a fifty-mile radius of the power plant. Nuclear power is not the answer to the

Philippines' energy needs, and anyway, *whose* needs are they, really?*

Foreign loans

How did a poor country like the Philippines finance these huge projects—the ports and other infrastructures, the export processing zones, the dams, the nuclear power plant? Through external aid and loans, of course.

Foreign loans have always been an important component in the economic development strategy of the Philippine government, and were so especially during the martial law years of the Marcos regime. Over the years, this borrowing has increased at a very critical rate.

For the agricultural export programs, credit schemes, infrastructures, new technology, etc., which ultimately have mainly benefitted the capitalists, the Philippines has incurred heavy debt. External debt by the end of 1986 reached $28.2 billion, 47 times the $599.5 million owed in 1965. By January 1988, the amount was $29 billion.[15] For a country the size of the Philippines, the amount is staggering. It is 4.4 times the Philippine national budget for 1987 and 81 percent of the expected GNP for 1987.[16] This pattern of heavy borrowing has actually been encouraged by the World Bank.

Because of perceived, or "created" needs, the World Bank, the International Monetary Fund and the Asian Development Bank, as well as foreign governments and their lending institutions, have continuously poured into the Philippines huge amounts of money for government projects and private businesses that have been guaranteed by the government.

Merely servicing these debts is draining our earnings. Already, interest payments eat up 44 percent of our national budget, requiring a tremendous outflow of foreign exchange.

---

* In 1987 the Aquino government decided to "mothball" this project, but continues to pay around $300 thousand *daily* to service the debt incurred in the construction of the nuclear reactor.

In early 1988, Solita Monsod, Minister of Planning, estimated that over the next six years the Philippines would be paying out approximately $18 billion in debt servicing costs and only getting $6 billion in new money. The burden of payments is actually borne by the people through excessive taxes upon income, real estate and landholdings, tolls for bridges and increased fares for public transportation. The poor are especially affected: with over 50 percent of the nation's export earnings siphoned off to pay debt servicing costs, and with a huge military budget, little is left for desperately needed government programs that could help the poor. Lending bodies impose austerity programs that eliminate support for cheaper food and better farm prices and that press to keep wages down—policies especially keenly felt by the poor. Increased emphasis on export activities to earn foreign exchange for paying the debt means that more and more land, and often the best land, tends to go into export crop production.

The Philippines, which is among the world's top ten borrowers, is the seventh largest debtor in the third world.[17] That is why economic and political activities in the country are so closely monitored by international lending institutions. The United States has particularly huge interests to lose if we do not get out of this debt mess.

There has been much debate over whether we should repay these debts. Part of the loans actually contributed to the personal benefit of Ferdinand Marcos and his cronies. These did not benefit the country at all, and lenders were well aware of this. A substantial portion of the debt was incurred under contracts later proven fraudulent. It appears thus far that the Aquino government intends to pay, which will inevitably require more loans, more taxes, more lives. Even if the gross national product increases, national debt will continue to be a most grave problem.

The debt problem is another example of how economic and political relationships in Philippine society allow the continued plunder of our resources and the intensifying oppression of our people. The debt problem is rooted in the tightening stranglehold on our economy by the rich and the powerful. For the ordinary Filipino, "development" is getting more vicious. To borrow a phrase from a Tribal Filipino, "development" is not our word![18]

The crisis and the prospects

Feudal bondage, foreign domination and the confluence of domestic and foreign interests have altogether stifled the promise of indigenous economic growth for the Philippines. How many generations of Filipinos have suffered poverty, ignorance, dependency and indebtedness? How long will our children and grandchildren have to serve their masters to pay for the debts of previous generations?

Governments never seem to learn from history. To resolve the crisis, the Philippine government is further opening up the economy for foreign involvement by providing generous incentives to foreign investors: cheap labor, no strikes, land accumulation, liberalized rules on profit expatriation, tax holidays and tax reductions. As in the past, these efforts will only increase economic dependency, indebtedness, depletion of resources, political intervention, cultural domination and internal conflict.

Science and technology have not resolved the interrelated problems that cause such terrible poverty. Neither did the final overthrow of the Marcos regime. The chronic consistency with which crisis after crisis occurs requires more than technological expertise, more than mastery of the game of politics within an international capitalist order, more than changes of government. New strategies will have to be defined for a just and equitable distribution of wealth, resources and power so that benefits shall accrue to all. Development will have to be understood as a liberating process of economic growth based on the primary principles of justice and human dignity.

But even in our anger and remorse we speak with courage and hope. We speak with willingness to learn from our history, to rediscover the inherent resources of our culture, to trace the liberating aspects in our nationalist tradition so that we may bravely confront the present. Even the educated elite landowners whose interests began to conflict with the Spanish colonizers had identified themselves with resistance movements and provided the articulation of their national will as a people. In spite of the inherent limitations of class interest, this heightened spirit of resistance eventually led to the Philippine Revolution of 1896. The oppressive situation provided the condition for the development of a revolutionary consciousness among the people. But the coming of the Americans changed the course of this consciousness.

While the Spaniards arrived to find geographically divided communities without a national consciousness, the Americans came upon a people strong in their determination to be free from the chains of domination. Met with widespread hostility, the Americans waged a war and systematic campaigns of suppression that became models for the Vietnam experience and, in recent years, for the anti-insurgency campaign in Mindanao.

> Aiming to isolate resistance movements from their mass base, the people who were suspected of supporting and protecting the revolutionaries were herded into designated concentration zones, outside of which properties were confiscated and destroyed. All persons caught outside the area were either shot on sight or arrested and imprisoned at the very least. Torture, water cure, burning of villages, massacre of village folks were rampant.[19]

Suppression, whether through such subtle influences pervading the cultural consciousness as education, the media and religion, or through the blatant use of force, has been a corollary strategy in the pursuit of economic interests. The government, for instance, announced the waging of a "total war" to quell the growing restlessness of the people. "Low Intensity Conflict" (LIC), a U.S. strategy used in other third-world countries, particularly in Latin America, is now being enforced: this is the fullest possible use of the political dimension that deliberately pits people against people in a war cast in East-West rhetoric, a war that is not really their own.

The United States continues to provide massive military aid to the Philippine government for its counter-insurgency campaigns in order to further promote and protect its own military bases and economic interests. This has devastating effects upon people and upon the prospects for true, people-oriented development.

If, indeed, changes are to occur, we will have to go back to the core of the issues at hand, primarily the issues of land and the related social relationships, of politics and of the culture bred by use of the land.

Farmers, for example, know that merely gaining land ownership is not the answer to their problems, but that economic development strategies should meet the need for more fundamental social and political changes. These strategies must involve provisions for support programs: realistic credit schemes, farm-to-market roads, services for the effective transfer of technology to ordinary people, cooperatives that are really owned and controlled by the people, the development of indigenous resources. The reform that is needed is that which would end feudal structures in the agrarian economy so that farmers can once again relate to the land and derive from it resources sufficient to their needs.

We Filipinos need to be able to redirect development priorities in order to become more truly independent and less vulnerable to the vagaries of an international economy that for centuries has forced us to become hostage to the dictates of foreign policies. We need to be able to control our resources and benefit from them ourselves so that there will be no more Filipino economic refugees in strange lands, and so that families

may live together again with dignity in the security
of their own homes.

Some encouraging examples of people's interaction
are happening at the grassroots level:

In Misamis Occidental, a church launched a
program providing alternative primary health care
to the community. The program involved education on health issues and related problems, on the
preparation and use of such self-reliant means as
herbal medicines, acupressure and acupuncture,
on nutrition and community child care. In the
course of education, reflection and organization,
other needs surfaced. Concerns broadened to
include consumer issues, breastfeeding, pollution
and advertising, among other things. Now, church
groups produce soap, oil and other indigenous
alternatives to the expensive consumer goods that
dominate the market.

A church in Maguindanao recently set up an
alternative education program for children of
farmers in the area. In workshop sessions, children
share the problems affecting their families, the
difficulties they face simply to be able to eat and
go to school. They learn practical skills in backyard
farming, care of animals, sanitation, health and
nutrition. They learn to appreciate their own
potential and resources as children of farmers as
they discuss what they can do together to improve
their living conditions.

In the Arakan Valley a group of Tribal Filipinos
has set up a cooperative farming program. They
have put together their resources—land, farming
tools, *carabaos*, themselves—in order to work more
systematically. Waste materials are combined to
make more organic fertilizers. They have come to
see that more people working together can
improve water control; more yields can provide
a better marketing position. Further, by working
together and sharing common concerns, they have

found more time to reflect on their own problems and to learn from and be strengthened by one another; they are more able to act together.

A church in Bukidnon served as a refugee center for people from the neighboring barrios who had been evacuated because of military operations in the area. Church members provided food, clothing and medicine to the refugees, and brought the emergency to the attention of churchpeople and government authorities.

In spite of the continuing suppression of economic and political rights, people are making their voices heard in various ways: through education and reflection groups, through organizing, by making protest statements, attending marches and rallies, lobbying in congress and in the senate, by forming solidarity linkages with support groups and concerned individuals. Students, professionals and churchpeople help in the articulation of people's aspirations. Not a few have given up positions of privilege to go to the countryside to teach, learn and even die in their commitment to be with the poor. In effect, we Filipinos are writing our own history.

So the elusive quest for development continues. It will be a long time before we can claim genuine development for our country and our people. But there are many signs of hope.

NOTES

1. Lichauco, Alejandro, *Towards a New Economic Order and the Conquest of Mass Poverty* (Quezon City: Lichauco, 1986), pp. 40-41.
2. Renato Constantino, *The Philippines: A Past Revisted* (Manila: 1975), p. 318
3. Ibid.
4. Renato Constantino, Letizia R. Constantino, *The Philippines: Continuing Past* (Quezon City: Foundation for Nationalist Studies, 1978), pp. 198ff.
5. Ibid., pp. 204 ff.
6. Rene E. Ofreneo, *Capitalism in Philippine Agriculture* (Quezon City: Foundation for Nationalist Studies, 1980), pp. 32-33.

7. Ernest Feder, *Perverse Development* (Quezon City: Foundation for Nationalist Studies, 1983), p. 3.
8. Ibid., pp. 161 ff.
9. Yashihara Kunio, *Philippine Industrialization* (Quezon City: Ateneo de Manila University Press, 1985), p. 33.
10. National Secretariat for Social Action (NASSA) Report, as cited by Feder.
11. *Timbangan*, Vol. IV, No. 2, (April and June, 1985).
12. Lorenzo M. Tañada, "BNPP: A Monument to Man's Folly, Pride and Refusal to Admit Mistakes," a speech delivered before cause-oriented groups at the Quezon City Sports Club, 1983.
13. Statement by Louis V. Nosenzo before the Commission on Appropriations Sub-Committee on Foreign Operations, Washington D.C., 8 February, 1978.
14. *op. cit.*, Tañada.
15. Interview with John Cavanagh, Washington, D.C., March 15, 1988.
16. IBON Data Bank facts and figures (Room 305, SCC Bldg., Sta. Mesa, Manila, Philippines).
17. Interview with John Cavanagh, *op. cit.*
18. Christian Conference of Asia, *No Place In the Inn: Voices of Minority People in Asia*, Workshop report, Urban-Rural Mission, May 1979.
19. Renato Constantino, *Neo-Colonial Identity and Counter-Consciousness* (London: Merrill Press, 1978), pp. 59 ff.

Editors' Note

According to some reports, Muslims in the Philippines number as many as five million—a substantial share of the country's total population of about fifty-seven million. A proud people, many of whom call themselves "Bangsa Moro," or the Moro People, they continue to resist, fiercely, attitudes and policies that in the past have sought their submission and absorption.

It should be remembered that while the Philippines is often called a "Christian nation," it is very much a part of the Malay world: racially, linguistically, and in important cultural ways. A tombstone on Mount Datu near Jolo bearing the date 710 A.H. (1310 C.E.) would seem to prove the existence of a Muslim community by that time. The thirteen ethno-linguistic groups that Filipino Muslims comprise are self-consciously a part of the Muslim majority of the other Southeast Asian island nations. "Filipino" is not a name that they have given themselves.

More than one hundred thousand Moros have died and approximately three hundred thousand have been displaced in bitter fighting in the southern islands over the last two decades. Centuries of resentment over the heavy-handed practices of "Christian" governments controlling them from the north, the loss of their ancestral lands to northern Filipino settlers, the destruction of their Islamic heritage and a sense of powerlessness, as well as the bitter fighting of the 1970s and 80s, have left a residue of bitterness. Difficult internal problems have added to the complexity of their situation. This is a horrendous context for the encouragement of dialogue and understanding between Muslims and Christians which, not surprisingly, is strongest in academic circles and in "people's movement" circles.

There are approximately seventy distinct tribal groups in the Philippines. Their leaders insist that no power governing that country has yet treated them with fairness or with proper respect for their human rights as individuals or communities. Hundreds of

thousands of hectares of ancestral lands have been
grabbed. Tribal peoples see big corporations taking
away the mineral wealth of the mountains they
consider a part of their heritage, with little benefit to
them. Loggers ravage their forests; once-productive
fields are submerged by the dammed waters of major
rivers, or lie idle in little-used national parks; agro-
industrial estates and military bases push them from
their land; their rivers and streams have become
yellow with eroded soil and pollution; their customs,
rituals and artistic skills are being exploited for
purposes of tourism and dollar-earning. Many Tribal
people have become scattered, marginalized groups in
cities and towns.

Tribal peoples' way of life has often been treated as
an oddity. They have repeatedly been the objects of
"objective" anthropological studies that have been
strangely silent concerning the critical issues
pertaining to their welfare. Their youth have been
caused to become estranged from their own people.

Since most Tribal peoples' ancestral areas have
become highly militarized, they have become targets
for harassment not only by right-wing vigilante and
fanatical groups, but even by the military. They are a
peaceful people, but some have finally taken up arms
in the name of "pangayaw," or last resort self-defense
against grave danger from the outside.

Theirs is the story of indigenous peoples
worldwide, whose customary laws for land use and
management have been disregarded; whose
traditional democratic systems for settling disputes,
judging and punishing wrongdoers, for reaching
decisions on all matters that affect their families and
communities, have been ignored. In place of these,
alien systems have been imposed which are less
democratic and usually terribly threatening.

CHRISTIANS, TRIBALS, MOROS

Filipinos in Search of Unity and Peace

Ed Maranan

In February 1986, the Filipino people ousted a dictatorship. It was a nonviolent process that has since been widely hailed as a "people's power revolution." It seemed then that after four hundred years of suffering under a succession of foreign and local tyrants, Filipinos were at last about to enjoy the full blessings of life in a climate of democracy and mutual respect.

Sadly, this was not to be so.

The Philippines remains a bloodily fragmented society. A new privileged elite has taken up where the old selfish oligarchs and bureaucrats left off. Wealthy and influential families continue to dominate politics.

While a fresh plague of graft and corruption stalks the halls of power, millions of Filipinos are sinking below the poverty line. Crimes against persons and property have not abated, but have worsened. Human rights violations are being committed with increasing frequency in the countryside, where military operations against armed rebels have been hurting innocent civilians.

Ed Maranan teaches Philippine studies at the University of the Philippines Asian Center. He is editor of *Asian Studies Journal*, and a member of the editorial board of *AGENDA*, a weekly publication. At present, he serves as vice-president of TABAK, a nationwide alliance involved in national minority concerns. During the Marcos period he was a political detainee for an extended period. A poet, playwright and fiction writer, he has won twenty-five national writing awards.

As if these problems were not enough for what used to be glowingly called "the only Christian country in Asia" and "the show window of democracy in the Far East," the issue of the country's national ethnic minorities, as well as that of the Muslims, endlessly simmers and now threatens to boil over.

A society divided

Both Tribal and Muslim Filipinos, seeing themselves as victims of many years of discrimination and neglect, have been asserting their right of self-determination in order to make the central government in Manila wake up to the gross injustices committed against them. In fact, a sizeable number of Tribal and Muslim Filipinos have chosen the more radical path of armed struggle to fight for what they believe are their legitimate claims. If the present government fails to put up a convincingly sincere program of peace and genuine development, then the possibility of a full-blown revolution becomes ever more real, like a dreaded storm cloud on the horizon.

The church in the Philippines has had a role in the unfolding of these events. For a long time, beginning with the Spanish colonial occupation, which lasted more than three hundred years, the church was regarded as a conservative institution that addressed itself only to religious and spiritual concerns. But the modern church in the Philippines has found itself slowly emerging into the forefront of the struggle for social justice. Under the Marcos dictatorship, elements within the church courageously took up the "preferential option for the poor." The church was involved in organizing institutions and movements that aimed to deal with the plight of the most disadvantaged sectors of the population, including the national ethnic minorities.

Among the organizations in which the church has had significant participation are the Episcopal Commission for Tribal Filipinos, the Commission for Christian-Muslim Dialogue, the People's Action for

Cultural Ties (PACT), the Ecumenical Movement for Justice and Peace, the Philippine Alliance of Human Rights Advocates, and the National Alliance for Philippine Minority Concerns. All these have something to do with working for the welfare of the country's national minorities, who now face the threat of growing militarization, and of whom many may even disappear completely from the land.

The national minorities in the Philippines are known by many names: ethnic Filipinos, aboriginals, Tribal people, hill tribes or highlanders, indigenous people, cultural communities, mountain folk, and even "non-Christians," "primitives," "savages" and "pagans."

Some people would classify Muslims among the national minorities, but this is resented by Muslims, who have always considered themselves a distinct society with their own history and culture. In fact, a growing sense of pride in their ethnic identity has led many Muslims to resist the label "Filipino," since this name, after all, was imposed by the Spanish *conquistadores* upon the inhabitants of the islands. It is on record that the Muslims were never conquered by Spanish colonialists. And not even the force of American arms at the turn of the century completely subjugated those fierce "heathens," as they were derisively called by Filipinos Christianized by the Spaniards and "re-Christianized" by Americans.

Thus has come about a society effectively divided into Christians, Tribals and Muslims.

Despite their being tagged "minorities," we are not dealing with just a few hundred thousand people. The Philippine minorities comprise a sizeable portion of the national population, close to six million out of a total of fifty-seven million inhabitants. The Muslims, for their part, account for another five million. Obviously, if such a large population chafes under unjust conditions brought about by structures, institutions and practices that have existed for many years, the looming crisis is of terrifying magnitude. It used to be that the main goal of these peoples was national integration, by which they could enjoy the same civil, political and economic rights as the majority. But in recent years, this goal has given way to more drastic demands such as autonomy (very close to self-rule), and even outright independence through secession or separation, which is the battle-cry of some Muslim groups.

Majority, minority

The national minority question in the Philippines involves relations between "mainstream society" (ethno-linguistic groups that are dominant in politics, economy and culture) and the "cultural minority" who comprise the different Tribal groups. The "majority" would also tend to consider Muslims a minority group.

The words "majority" and "minority" represent a tragic condition in human society not only in the Philippines, but anywhere that conflict has become the common lot on account of ethnic, racial, religious, communal or territorial differences and interests.

As understood in the Philippines, "majority" refers to those who live in the productive lowlands, the rural population centers and the urbanized areas. Most of the positions in the government, from the national down to the village level, are occupied by people of the majority. They have full representation in all three branches of the government, or else they are elected or appointed to its varied posts and sinecures.* The bulk of the armed forces, the police and the paramilitary units are made up of people of the majority. Companies and factories are owned by or employ people of the majority. Although many of the majority are themselves poor, it is majority people who are more likely to enjoy the benefits of education, social services, health and welfare programs, and the fruits of technology and twentieth-century living.

In short, the majority controls politics, monopolizes commerce and dictates culture. It is also, incidentally, predominantly Christian.

---

* An office or position with financial reward, but for which few or no duties are required.

On the other hand, the "minority" refers to those who occupy the interior hills and mountains, the barren strips of coasts and hinterlands, the isolated valleys and tropical rain forests. They live in huts whose architecture has not changed in hundreds of years, or in makeshift lean-tos, hovels, longhouses and even cave dwellings. They are prone to a host of diseases and suffer the highest mortality rates. Many of them have never seen a classroom. Long the stewards of an enormous ecosystem that could potentially sustain a population many times its present number, minority people are now threatened with extinction by the onslaught of "progress" and "civilization."

Logging concessions owned by local capitalists and the agro-industrial empires of giant multinationals gobble up their ancestral domains. For years, mining companies have extracted gold, copper and other minerals from the mountains of the Gran Cordillera range of northern Luzon, where the Igorots have lived for centuries. But so far, the only economic benefit the Igorots have received is the pittance paid out to them as locally hired miners. Most of the profits go into the coffers of the big businessmen and foreign investors who own these mines. The Igorots remain largely impoverished. Only a few, especially those who have risen in politics and struck it rich under the Marcos regime, have escaped the curse of poverty brought about by underdevelopment.

On the island of Mindoro, an attempt has been made to start coal mining operations in the land of the Mangyans. Like other groups in the country, Mangyans now risk being pushed down to the coastal settlements, where land and resources are already in the hands of Christian settlers, or forced back further inland where hunting and farming can hardly be sustained. Over the years, the Mangyans have lost more than 135,000 hectares of land to concessionaires of mines and forests, as well as to ranchers.

In an even more precarious situation are the Bataks of Palawan. Only a few hundred remain out of the several thousand who used to inhabit the tropical rain forest of this island province in the western Philippines. Disease, malnutrition and hunger brought about by the depletion of their food sources have killed most of them. Logging roads eat deep into their forest sanctuary. They have become as vulnerable as a threatened species of animal flushed out of its natural territory.

An even more dramatic case of the exploitation of minorities is the fate of the so-called Tasaday, the "stone-age cave-dwellers" of the Philippines. Announced to the world during the early part of the Marcos regime as one of the most important anthropological "finds" of the century, it was recently claimed that the Tasaday phenomenon was an elaborate hoax[*] dreamed up by a Marcos bureaucrat who was also an oligarch with possible interest in the Tasaday mountains, forest and mineral resources.

The United States, it seems, has also played a role in making life miserable for the Filipino minorities. A recent report in the church-based "Philippine News and Features" tells of the Negritos and Zambals of Central Luzon, whose ancestral lands were taken over long ago by the sprawling military bases of the U.S. armed forces in the Pacific. These mountains and valleys straddling two provinces have been turned into bombing and shooting ranges by the Americans. War games constantly disrupt the people's lives, armored vehicles run roughshod across plants and vegetation and the rumble of tanks and the roar of warplanes continually terrify the animals.

Some minority people are even subjected to a modern form of slavery called the "tabong" system. This has been the cruel lot of the Dumagats, who inhabit the deep forest region of the Sierra Madre mountains in Luzon. In the distant past the Dumagats lived by the sea, where fish were abundant. Migrating Tagalogs (the leading majority group in the Philippines) pushed them up into the mountain fastnesses, where they survived

---

[*] This dispute continues, seemingly with all but the Tasaday people themselves benefiting.

by hunting game and gathering rattan. The tabong
system involves Tagalog middlemen. The Dumagats
sell their game and rattan to these middlemen, or
tabongs, who pay for the goods with a few kilograms
of rice and a small amount of salt. The exchange is
unfair because meat and rattan can fetch high prices
in the lowlands and rattan is a popular export product.
The Dumagats, however, do not know much about
commercial transactions and they put their trust in the
tabongs, who decree what the terms of exchange should
be. The tabongs deceive the Dumagats by overpricing
their rice and salt to the extent that the Dumagats end
up in debt and are forced to gather more rattan, which
somehow never seems to be enough to cover their
"debt." The Dumagat debtor is then "owned" by the
tabong, who can sell him and his debt to another
tabong. Even the "debts" of dead relatives are added
on, thus ensuring the Dumagat's continuing
enslavement.

During the Marcos regime, the government claimed
"development" to be the basis of its policies towards
the national minorities. But this claim was actually an
ill-concealed attempt to either control or sell out the
rich natural resources found in the Tribal people's
ecological habitat.

Another reason for the forcible intrusion into the
territory of minority people was counter-insurgency.
During the Marcos period, militarization became a by-
word. This simply meant extensive combat operations,
both in the countryside and the highland areas
inhabited by the Tribal peoples. Their lands were
invaded, either to deprive the rebels of a mass base
of support or to enable big business to set up enterprises
of forest and farm products. For example, on the island
of Mindanao, where hundreds of thousands of hectares
are devoted to agribusiness owned by foreign firms
such as Dole and Del Monte, Tribal people have been
forced out of their ancient land and gathered together
in "strategic hamlets."

A similarly tragic fate has befallen peasant settlers
from other islands who came to Mindanao in search

of enough good land to till and the peace and quiet of the countryside. These settlers have seen their dreams shattered by rabid anti-communist vigilante formations and fanatic cults (both encouraged and armed by the Philippine military) that have tortured, raped or murdered hundreds and forced thousands to become refugees from their own land. Now, both peasant settlers and the indigenous Tribal people of Mindanao—called the Lumad—are feeling the brunt of intensified militarization in the name of "development" and anti-communism.

So bad has the situation become for the minority people in Mindanao that "reservation sites" are being proposed. In the province of Agusan, one area of about sixteen hectares is being eyed for some ten thousand displaced people from various tribes. The scheme is supposed to "guard the unique heritage of the cultural highlanders and uphold the government's thrust towards its preservation and advancement." Others see in this scheme only a makeshift solution to the intensifying conflict between the minority people and capitalist interests. They ask: what is to stop the government from restricting entire communities of Tribal people to well-defined "reservation sites" of a few hectares, while the rest of the mountains, forests, valleys and plains are taken over by multinationals, military installations (Filipino or American), logging operators, agribusinessmen and well-connected land speculators?

The sad history of the Native American people seems to have been conveniently forgotten by those who propose "reservation sites" for the Philippine Tribal people!

The "Moro" Question

The Muslim, or Moro, Question is altogether a different issue, and perhaps more complex. Its implications for the future of Philippine society are awesome. If left unresolved, or if resolved through continued war, this issue could lead to the division of the Philippine state: one state for the Christians, another for the Muslims.

Both Muslims and Christians in the Philippines, particularly the leaders on both sides, swear that the problem has nothing to do with religion. This may be true, for indeed, the basic complaint of the Mindanao Muslims is that for a very long time the central government in Manila has neglected the welfare of the five million Muslims in the south, and has in fact abetted the steady erosion of Muslim control over their own territorial interests. But apart from the greed of politicians and big capitalists staking out huge claims on the fertile island of Mindanao, Muslim society itself has been beset by an internal problem of inequality. The traditional elite is composed of wealthy families that include a fair share of the country's political warlords. In this sense, the situation is no better than in Christian society, where the majority seem to be forever poor while the affluent few lord it over them from the top of the proverbial pyramid. In this sense, perhaps, religion is not an issue.

The history of Islam in the Philippines cannot, however, be ignored. Long before Christianity came into the picture, parts of the country were already under the influence of Islam brought by traders and religious teachers from Southeast Asia. Despite the successful Spanish pacification program in the islands of Luzon and in the Visayan island group, European Christianity did not make much headway in Mindanao. A series of bloody wars only served to embitter Muslims' feelings against Christians, both the Spanish *conquistadores* and their newly converted native mercenaries. The Spaniards fought the Muslims in the Philippines for more than three hundred years and failed to repeat the victory they had won in driving the Moors out of Spain. (The word "Moro" was used by the Spaniards for the Philippine Muslims, a reference to the Moors, their rivals in the Mediterranean.)

It was only during the American occupation of the Philippines in the 1900s that Muslim resistance was brought under some semblance of control. The Moro

Campaign was as bloody an episode in Mindanao as was the Philippine-American War in Luzon and the Visayas. Using all the expertise gained from the U.S. Army's war against Native Americans on the American frontier, the United States succeeded in its "pacification campaign" in the Philippines—including the south. It even devised a special weapon to bring the natives to heel: the famous Colt .45 automatic pistol is said to have been crafted for the specific purpose of stopping the fierce Moro warrior dead in his tracks in his headlong attack against the foreign intruder.

The effects of the American occupation government in Muslim Mindanao are still being felt. In a well-researched article by minority rights advocate Rene Agbayani ("The Bangsa Moro Struggle," *Diliman Review*, 1987), the colonial strategy of the U.S. Government is described as having been that of classic divide-and-rule, through:

1. a series of migration programs for the peasants of Luzon and the Visayas, which gave land to these people (and eased agrarian unrest in the Christian areas), but in the process took ancestral lands away from the Bangsa Moro (the Muslim nation) and the hill tribes;
2. the introduction of large-scale investment, exploration and exploitation by Filipino and American capitalists; and
3. the creation of a bureaucracy led by Christian natives, with the help of some Bangsa Moro elite families, to make colonization trouble-free.

This was the ominous beginning of the so-called "Moro Question" or "Mindanao Problem."

At present, according to Agbayani, the Bangsa Moro control only about seventeen percent of their original homeland, and most of these areas are mountainous and infertile. Marketing facilities and infrastructures are absent or inadequate. Thus the majority of Moros suffer the same predicament in which seventy to eighty percent of all Filipinos presently find themselves.

The 1972 declaration of martial law deepened the crisis in Mindanao. For many years, armed Christian settlers had been attacking Muslim settlements with the open or tacit support of the Armed Forces of the Philippines. The Muslims started to fight back, organizing self-defense units which were later to evolve into the present-day Moro National Liberation Front (MNLF). The Marcos government's campaign against the MNLF resulted in tens of thousands of Muslim casualties and turned hundreds of thousands of Muslims into refugees who were either scattered all over Mindanao or fled to Sabah (North Borneo), where they have remained.

The MNLF fought furiously, but by 1976 the war had reached a stalemate. The Philippine government was forced to negotiate with the MNLF through the Organization of Islamic Conferences. The Tripoli Agreement, which was signed on December 23, 1976, called for the creation of a single Muslim Autonomous Zone (MAZ) in thirteen Mindanao provinces but within the jurisdiction of the Republic of the Philippines. It also called for the withdrawal of the Armed Forces of the Philippines. The Bangsa Moro would provide for its own autonomous security forces.

Because the agreement would have meant a sizable reduction in its political and economic control of the resource-rich island of Mindanao, the Marcos government eventually went back on its word and resumed hostilities against the MNLF. It even sponsored its own version of "autonomy" in two regions of the island and worked to create a rift within the ranks of the MNLF. The MNLF was later to split into three rival groups, each with its own strategy against the Philippine government and its own autonomy plan for Bangsa Moro. The main MNLF, however, under the leadership of Nur Misuari, remains the strongest and the most militant of these groups. It recently figured in negotiations with the Aquino government over a substantial autonomy set-up for the Muslims, but the continuing stalemate between the government and the Misuari people has again raised the spectre of renewed fighting. The MNLF has even mentioned the possibility of shifting its demand from mere autonomy to outright secession, which was the original dream of idealistic Muslim freedom fighters, who were utterly frustrated with the policies of past Philippine government administrations.

The MNLF has demanded that the Bangsa Moro, through its popular organizations, should determine the structure of the proposed autonomous Muslim territory and also that any agreement should involve the Christians in Mindanao as well as non-Muslim, non-Christian Tribal people. After all, while these three groups may represent diverse religions or world views, customs, laws and codes of conduct, they have for ages occupied one bountiful land and shared a common history of exploitation by the rich and powerful. It has been said, in fact, that since the newly elected members of congress representing Mindanao are mostly the old style of politicos from the landed gentry and *comprador* class, they can hardly be expected to defend the interests of the poor. But while the Muslims of Mindanao are represented in both houses of congress (whether they are the representatives of their people is another matter), and have themselves been appointed to a number of positions, the Tribal Filipinos do not enjoy the same degree of participation in the legal political process.

It seems today that the government of Corazon Aquino has lost the revolutionary momentum that brought it to power. The spirit of "re-democratization" was supposed to have wrought sweeping changes throughout all of Philippine society by means of popular empowerment and the overhaul of corrupt and inhuman structures—particularly the bureaucracy and the military—and through the opening up of social and economic opportunities to the most disadvantaged sectors and classes. The new age that was expected to rise out of the ruins of a land devastated by greed and oppression could finally have provided solutions to the age-old problems of the Tribal Filipinos and the Filipino Muslims.

Recent events, however, prove that the basic problems of the Filipino people remain deeply rooted. Workers are going through one of the worst anti-labor eras in the country's history. Peasants have been massacred on Manila's streets as well as in the countryside. The number of urban poor is increasing as the world of slums grows. Meanwhile, Muslims and Tribal Filipinos continue to face an uncertain future. Their tales of exploitation and repression may be only occasionally mentioned in the media, but they are frequently discussed in academic and advocacy circles.

In defense of the land: the ancestral domain

The dreams of the minority people of the Philippines have been articulated time and again by those who have led or inspired them in their struggle. These dreams have invariably taken the shape of retaining and defending the ancestral domain.

A Mangyan elder from the beleaguered island of Mindoro has left us a fragment of the Mangyan worldview:

> The land. . . what I know of it is that God alone owns the land. He made it for all to use. Why do people now claim it as their own? Why is it that now, when you cannot pay these people money, they own the land? This way, we have no hope. But I will continue tilling my land. It is my place and I will never leave it.

The most celebrated of ethnic declarations in recent memory belongs to the Kalinga chieftain Macli-ing Dulag, who was assassinated in 1981 by elements of the Philippine Armed Forces for having led the opposition to the World Bank-funded Chico River Dam project:

> Apu Kabunian, lord of us all, gave us life in the world to live human lives. And where shall we obtain life? From the land. To work the land is

an obligation, not merely a right. In tilling the land, you possess it. And so, land is a grace that must be nurtured. To enrich it and make it bear fruit is the eternal exhortation of Apu Kabunian to all his children. Land is sacred, and is beloved. From its womb springs our Kalinga life.

How universal, it seems, is the attitude of traditional cultures towards the sanctity of land as a communal treasure. Dulag's words remind us of the Native American Chief Seattle's declaration in a letter he wrote in 1854, which read in part:

Every part of this earth is sacred to my people. Every shining pine needle, every sandy shore, every mist in the dark woods, every clearing and every humming insect is holy in the memory and experience of my people. The sap which courses through the trees carries the memories of the red man. . . . This we know: the earth does not belong to man. Man belongs to the earth.

For both Tribal Filipinos and the Filipino Muslims, the organizing principle of their present political program is self-determination. They insist on the right to govern themselves according to their centuries-old institutions of law and moral order, as well as the right to partake more fully of the economic benefits derived from their ancestral domain.

Peaceful co-existence among Christians, Tribals and Moros will become a reality when the political elite wielding the powers of the state begins to realize that the problem of peace and harmony goes beyond the religious question and has its deep roots in the poisoned soil of poverty. This poverty represents the dead weight of centuries, first nurtured by colonialism, next made to flourish by social inequality, and now growing uncontrollably as it is fertilized, as it were, by the illusion that "all is well, the dictatorship has fallen."

The alternative to such peaceful co-existence would be a tragedy of cataclysmic proportions—a tragedy which, sadly, is already beginning to happen.

Editors' Note

A thoughtful reading of Helen Graham's rich, carefully crafted chapter deepens our realization of how far we have wandered from the Shalom Way and how serious is our global predicament, the Philippine crisis in particular. We are reminded that it is not enough to struggle against the visible manifestations of militarization and violence, but that it is also essential that we deal with the attitudes and values that are their driving force.

As you read this chapter, take note of how your own awareness as a person of faith may deepen concerning peace and regarding the question, what is true peace? How many new dimensions of the meaning of shalom can you identify? What might these dimensions mean, concretely, for Filipinos? For Americans?

This section of the book should be of unusual value as a basis for small group reflection and discussion. Portions may also be adapted for liturgical use.

THE THINGS THAT MAKE FOR PEACE

Helen R. Graham, M.M.

> And when [Jesus] drew near and saw the city he wept over it, saying, "Would that even today you knew *the things that make for peace!* But now they are hid from your eyes. For the days shall come upon you, when your enemies will cast up a bank about you and surround you, and hem you in on every side, and dash you to the ground, you and your children within you, and they will not leave one stone upon another in you; because you did not know the time of your visitation.
>
> Luke 19:41-44; italics added.

Descending the Mount of Olives, one comes upon a small tear-shaped church called Dominus Flevit (meaning "the Lord wept"). Medieval pilgrims had designated a certain rock on the Mount of Olives as the place where Jesus wept over Jerusalem, and the Franciscans built this chapel nearby. Inside the chapel, a large semicircular window behind the altar provides a panoramic view of the Old City of Jerusalem (which means "a foundation of peace or prosperity"). The chapel also contains a mosaic reflecting Jesus's words: "O Jerusalem, Jerusalem. . . . How often would I have gathered your children together as a hen gathers her

Helen Graham, a Maryknoll Sister who for many years has specialized in "preparation for ministry," teaches at the Sisters' Formation Institute and St. Mary's Theologate in Quezon City, and at Ateneo de Manila. An Old Testament scholar, she did her major Hebrew studies at Harvard University.

brood under her wings, but you would not" (Luke
13:34). Since the seventh century, the city's skyline has
been dominated by the majestic golden Dome of the
Rock. This mosque, the first major sanctuary built by
Islam, occupies the place where the Temple once stood.
Standing at the chapel window, looking out at the Old
City, it is not difficult to enter into the deep sadness
of the Lucan passage. The mind wanders, and as the
buildings across the Kidron valley start to blur, one
can hear Jesus speaking to the world: "Would that even
today you knew the things that make for peace!"

Without doubt the world in which we live today
is threatened much more seriously than ancient
Jerusalem ever was: threatened by global problems
that have arisen because of the interdependence of
people and societies, and by the interconnection of
happenings in various fields. Global problems, as
distinct from local, national or regional situations, affect
people in almost all parts of the world and call for
global-level solutions.[1]

In the Philippines, some of these worldwide problems
are manifested in the following ways:

• a majority of the population living without a
minimum acceptable level of health, sanitation, food
and shelter, while there is little or no social services
budget to fill the gap;
• an economy struggling to recover from two years
of negative growth rate (1984-85), while bearing the
burden of servicing a $29 billion foreign debt;
• rapid population growth (2.5 percent in 1986) with
its corresponding decline in per capita income (16
percent in the period 1980-1986);
• rapid deforestation at the rate of 1.2 percent every
year, which has resulted in the reduction of the forest
area from 15 million hectares in 1969 to 6 million
in 1987 (a hectare is approximately 2.5 acres);
• almost two decades of civil war involving the
Armed Forces of the Philippines against the National
Democratic Front (NDF), the New People's Army
(NPA), and Muslim groups in the south, with

hundreds of non-involved civilians suffering the consequences;

• growing militarization, which has led to a five-fold increase in the nation's armed forces in a decade (1972-1984): from 62,000 to more than 250,000 persons; forces that have spent most of their thirty-nine year history fighting and killing other Filipinos; and

• the proliferation of right-wing vigilante groups in various parts of the country engaged in the harassment, intimidation, torture and even execution of any who are suspected of supporting the revolutionary movements.

These are some of the trends that demonstrate a lack of well-being (shalom) in the world community in general, and in the Philippines in particular. Human beings have the capacity to produce both "bad" and "good." The "bad," in terms of direct violence, is increasing and becoming qualitatively more destructive. While "good" is indeed being produced, for example, in the areas of nutrition, world health and education, the world is so structured that production is geared toward economic demand rather than toward the satisfaction of fundamental human needs. Consequently, more and more people in poor countries have fewer and fewer of their basic needs satisfied.[2] What, then, lies ahead for human societies?

Reading the Lucan passage (19:41-44) against this background of global crisis, we can well imagine Jesus addressing all of us: "Would that even today you knew the things that make for peace!"

What, indeed, are the elemental things that make for peace? What is peace? There are no simple answers to these questions, yet the Scriptures call upon us, as they called upon our ancestors in the faith, to "seek peace (shalom), and pursue it" (Psalm 34:15). We turn, therefore, to our religious heritage, to the Scriptures, which embody the collective wisdom of millennia of faith in "Yahweh shalom" ("the Lord is Peace"—Judges 6:24). Let us make an effort to grasp something of the understanding of peace enshrined in its pages.

The meaning of shalom

To inquire into the meaning of the biblical concept of shalom requires that we go well beyond dictionary definitions, particularly taking into account its socio-historical context.[3]

More than 350 occurrences of the word "shalom" and its derivatives are found in a series of texts written mostly in Hebrew* and covering a span of thousands of years, from the twelfth century to the second century B.C.E.† During that time span, Israel went through three major phases of socio-cultural and economic history: as free agrarians engaged in subsistence farming in the central highlands of Canaan (1250-1050 B.C.E.); as peasant farmers whose surplus (made possible by such technological innovations as iron tools, rock terracing and lime-slaked cisterns for water storage) had been siphoned off by the increasingly powerful state bureaucracy (586-100 B.C.E.); and as a dispersed people who had lost their independence to a succession of foreign empires.[4]

Shalom as peace

The English word "peace," which ultimately derives from the Latin *pax*, does not adequately reflect the richness of meaning conveyed by the Hebrew "shalom." Shalom (*salom* in Hebrew), which comes from the verb "to be complete, whole," is an expression of a very comprehensive nature. Shalom is a prime example of a word with multiple possibilities of meaning (see endnote 3). For this reason, its interpretation calls for various strategies.

---

* A small percentage of the texts are in Aramaic. The Hebrew Bible was translated into Greek in the third century B.C.E. This translation, which is called the Septuagint (LXX), contains seven additional books that Protestants call the Apocrypha and Roman Catholics call deuterocanonical books.

† "B.C.E." is more commonly used than "B.C." today, along with "C.E." rather than "A.D." It means Before the Common Era, while C.E. stands for Common Era.

Among these strategies is what the philosopher Paul Ricoeur calls the "strategy of ordinary language," of which the main aim is communication. This involves the tactic of limiting or reducing the many possibilities of meaning, thus achieving greater clarity. The "strategy of ordinary language" would apply to the large number of straightforward occurrences of shalom in the Hebrew Bible where the meaning is easily discerned. When Qohelet (or Ecclesiastes) uses the word shalom as the antithesis of the Hebrew word for war in Ecclesiastes 3:8, it is clear that shalom here means peace as the opposite of war. When we are told that Sisera, the commanding general of the King of Hazor, took refuge in the tent of Heber the Kenite because "there was *shalom* between Jabin...and the house of Heber the Kenite" (Judges 4:17), we understand that there was a relationship between the King of Hazor and the household of Heber the Kenite such that Sisera could expect protection.

But when we read in Psalm 85 that

Kindness and fidelity will meet,
 justice and *shalom* will embrace,
Fidelity shall sprout from the earth,
 and justice lean down from heaven (vs. 13),

we are at a loss as to how to interpret shalom. Likewise, when Second Isaiah, the great unknown prophet of the Exile, says,

Then right will settle in the wilderness,
 and justice will inhabit the orchard,
and the fruit of justice will be *shalom*,
 and the yield of justice quiet security forever
(Isaiah 32:16-17),

how are we to understand shalom?

What is involved in these last two examples is the use of a word in a way that is different from the way ordinary language usually uses words. We are dealing here with what Ricoeur calls the "strategy of metaphor." This strategy makes creative use of the fact that words are open to multiple meanings. Traditional rhetoric

understood a metaphor to be merely a figure of speech.
That is, it was to borrow a word and substitute it for
a potential proper name which could be used in its
place. The metaphor, in that sense, brought with it no
new information, but was merely a decorative element.
Ricoeur reminds us, however, that metaphors also have
the power to break through old meanings and establish
new ones.[5]

Shalom as well-being

At its root, shalom carries the sense of "well-being,"
a well-being that extends into the personal, social,
political and economic realms. This means that on a
personal level, one might inquire after the health
(shalom) of another. Thus Jacob asks, concerning Laban,
"Is it well (shalom) with him?" (Genesis 29:6). And
Joseph asks his brothers about their father, Jacob,
saying, "Is your father well (shalom), the old man of
whom you spoke? Is he still alive?" (Genesis 43:27).*
But shalom can also be used to speak metaphorically
of the health or well-being of a whole people.
Concerning his opponents, the prophet Jeremiah
complains:

> They have healed the wound of my people lightly,
>   saying, "Peace, peace"
> when there is no peace. (Jeremiah 6:14; cf. 8:11)

One would have to study the socio-historical context
in which Jeremiah lived to appreciate fully what the
"wound" of his people was. But whatever the wound
was, the prophet asserts that it is bad medical practice
to simply keep treating symptoms, to heal superficially.

Shalom as covenantal relationship

In other uses, shalom denotes a relationship and is
frequently found in connection with the making of a
covenant:

---

* At this stage in the story Joseph was still unknown to his brothers; that
is why the question was "Is *your* father well...?"

And Joshua made peace with them [the
Gibeonites] and made a covenant with them, to
let them live; and the leaders of the congregation
swore to them. (Joshua 9:15)

In 1 Kings 5:12 we are told that "there was peace
between Hiram and Solomon," and in 1 Samuel 7:14,
that "there was also peace between Israel and the
Amorites." Linguistically, these statements are exactly
the same, with the exception of the proper nouns. But
when these texts are read in their socio-historical
contexts they convey two entirely different situations.
In the latter case we are dealing with the strategic
joining of forces between two former enemies because
of a greater threat, the Philistines. In the former case,
Hiram and Solomon enter into mutually beneficial trade
relations at the expense of most of their people, who
are consequently subjected to forced labor and to
exactions of their grain and oil. The environment also
suffered, because Solomon imported all the cedar and
cypress he wanted for his many building projects (1
Kings 5:10).

In the sixth century B.C.E., the prophet Ezekiel spoke
of a "covenant of peace" that Yahweh would make with
Israel: "I will make with them a covenant of peace and
banish wild beasts from the land, so that they may
dwell securely in the wilderness and sleep in the
woods" (Ezekiel 34:25). And again, "I will make a
covenant of peace with them; it shall be an everlasting
covenant with them; and I will bless them and multiply
them, and will set my sanctuary in the midst of them
forevermore" (Ezekiel 37:26). A similar promise was
spoken by Second Isaiah toward the end of the
Babylonian period: "...my steadfast love shall not
depart from you, and my covenant of peace shall not
be removed..." (Isaiah 54:10).

Shalom as prosperity

Individual and group prosperity are referred to in
two Psalm passages. In a prayer for the accession of
a new king to the throne, the congregation prays for

bountiful harvests: "Let the mountains bear prosperity (shalom) for the people, and the hills, in righteousness!" (Ps. 72:3). In another prayer, an Israelite struggles in Job-like fashion with life's paradox: "For I was envious...when I saw the prosperity (shalom) of the wicked" (Ps. 73:3).

Other uses

Shalom is even used in one instance with reference to a battle. In 2 Samuel 11:7, David asks about the shalom of Joab, the shalom of the people and the shalom of the war. (In the RSV, this is translated, "...how Joab was doing, and how the people fared, and how the war prospered.")

It is clear, therefore, that both the literary and socio-historical contexts must be taken into account in the interpretation of a concept like "shalom." Whether the reader comes from an industrial or an industrializing agrarian society will have a bearing on how a text is read and interpreted. The social location of the reader, as well as the events described, also play vital roles.

Since Israel was an agrarian society, one of its major concerns was land and its produce. It is therefore not surprising to find that shalom is envisioned in much of the Bible as the conditions that make for agrarian productivity shared by all. The absence of those conditions is peacelessness, which calls down God's judgment.

New Testament meanings

We turn now to the New Testament, which employs the Greek term *eirene* for the Hebrew word shalom. *Eirene* originally meant simply the opposite of war. The term could also mean the positive social experience of harmony and order. Contact with the Hebrew shalom expanded the Greek term to include the notions of well-being, happiness and health. Thus the flourishing condition of the early church is described in Acts as one of peace: "So the church throughout all Judea and Galilee and Samaria had peace and was built up..."

(9:31). And peace is linked with joy and righteousness in Paul's letter to the Romans: "For the reign of God does not mean food and drink but righteousness and peace and joy in the Holy Spirit" (14:17). Many of the epistles use *eirene* (peace) along with *charis* (grace) as a greeting (Romans 1:7; 1 Corinthians 1:3; 2 Corinthians 1:2; Galatians 1:3; Philippians 1:2, etc.).

Perhaps these examples are enough to demonstrate the comprehensive nature of the biblical concept of shalom with its strong emphasis on physical and social well-being and on material prosperity.

"Then I will give shalom in the land. . ."

In the concluding exhortation of the section of the Book of Leviticus commonly referred to as the Holiness Code (Chapters 17-26), shalom is described as a material blessing bestowed on the land by Yahweh. The passage reads:

> "If you walk in my statutes and observe my commandments and do them, then I will give you your rains in their season, and the land shall yield its increase, and the trees of the field shall yield their fruit. And your threshing shall last to the time of vintage, and the vintage shall last to the time for sowing; and you shall eat your bread to the full, and dwell in your land securely. Then I will give peace (shalom) in the land, and you shall lie down, and none shall make you afraid; and I will remove evil beasts from the land, and the sword shall not go through your land." (Leviticus 26:3-6).

In this passage a cause-and-effect relationship is posited between walking in Yahweh's statutes,[*] observing God's commandments and doing them, and the onset of the annual rains essential for the production of grain, wine and oil.[†] A bountiful harvest is promised,

---

[*] See also Luke 1:79, where the hymn of Zechariah uses similar dynamic imagery: ". . .guide our feet into the way of peace."

[†] I am assuming olive trees, but fruit trees are also possible.

so bountiful that the time of the grain threshing (spring) will last until the time of vintage (early autumn) and the time of vintage will overtake the sowing (winter). Abundance of food for all means dwelling securely in the land. It is only when there is abundance of food for all that Yahweh bestows the blessing of shalom in the land, so that its inhabitants can sleep without fear of attack from wild beasts or the sword of war.

Here we may sense something of the *concreteness* of Israel's understanding of "the things that make for peace."

This same side-by-side placement of the themes of obedience to Yahweh's law, agricultural productivity and the absence of war also appears in a passage traced to the last days of the Babylonian exile:

It shall come to pass in the latter days
    that the mountain of the house of the Lord
shall be established as the highest of the mountains,
    and shall be raised up above the hills;
and peoples shall flow to it,
    and many nations shall come, and say:
"Come, let us go up to the mountain of the Lord,
    to the house of the God of Jacob;
    that he may teach us his ways
    and we may walk in his paths."
For out of Zion shall go forth the law [Heb., *torah*]
    and the word of the Lord from Jerusalem.
He shall judge between many peoples
    and shall decide for strong nations afar off;
and they shall beat their swords into
    ploughshares,
    and their spears into pruning hooks;
nation shall not lift up sword against nation,
    neither shall they learn war any more;
but they shall sit every one under their own vine
    and under their own fig tree,
    and none shall make them afraid;
    for the mouth of the Lord of hosts has spoken.
(Micah 4:1-4; cf. Isa. 2:2-4)

This passage envisions the conversion of the nations, "the self-contained systems of security and meaning," as Walter Brueggemann so aptly describes them,[6] the conversion of the nations to Yahweh (vs. 2). The great judgment scene to take place on the top of "the mountain of the Lord" will inaugurate a policy change by which the propagators of arms proliferation will submit themselves to Yahweh's *torah* and will walk in the paths defined by Yahweh's word! As a result of this shift in consciousness and realignment of priorities, destructive armaments will be transformed into instruments of production: "and they shall beat their swords into ploughshares and their spears into pruning hooks; nation shall not lift up sword against nation, neither shall they learn war any more" (vs. 3).

The final scene of the Micah passage depicts security and peace as each person sits "under their own vine and their own fig tree" without fear of confiscation, attack or other form of state encroachment on agrarian productivity. This scene recalls the passage of Leviticus 26:3-6, which also links dwelling in the land without fear, and food sufficiency: "You shall eat your bread to the full, and dwell in your land securely . . . and none shall make you afraid." The poet betrays an extraordinary insight that seems to escape present-day policymakers: there is an intimate connection between war and hunger. War produces hunger. And, we might add, hunger can produce war. Walking in Yahweh's statutes, observing God's commandments and doing them is what makes for peace, i.e., is what brings Yahweh's blessing upon the land in the form of agricultural bounty and security against attack from wild beasts and the sword of war.

Remarkable early social legislation in the Bible

As we look through the statutes and commandments of Yahweh contained in the three major legal collections of the Pentateuch,[*] we are struck by how much of the

---

[*] The so-called Covenant Code of Exodus 20:22 - 23:9; the Deuteronomic Code of Deuteronomy 12-26; and the Holiness Code of Leviticus 17-26.

earlier legislation was social in nature. A quick survey
of the material yields the following:

- laws that express Yahweh's gracious concern for
the poor, so that those responsible for justice are
warned not to pervert the justice that is due to the
poor in their legal suits (Exodus 23:6; see also 22:5;
23:10);
- laws that prohibit violent ill-treatment, exploitation or molestation of those most vulnerable in
society: the widow, the fatherless and the stranger
(Exodus 22:21-23; see also Deuteronomy 24:17; 14:28,
29; 16:10-13, etc.);
- laws that attempt to humanize somewhat the
ancient institution of slavery (Exodus 21:2-11; cf.
Deuteronomy 15:12-18, etc.);
- laws that recognize that indebtedness is the major
cause of property loss and the loss of freedom
through slavery, and thus prohibit taking interest
when lending to a co-Israelite (Exodus 22:25-27;
Deuteronomy 23:20 etc.);
- to further prevent the poverty resulting from
indebtedness, every seventh year to be declared a
year of release from debts (Deuteronomy 15:1-11);
- the Sabbath command, as presented in the Book
of Deuteronomy, speaks of the liberation of all (even
the work animals!) for one day a week as an effective
remembrance of the Israelite liberation from the
slavery of Egypt (Deuteronomy 5:12-15; cf. Exodus
20:8-10);
- and finally, the Jubilee year, a multiple of Sabbath
years, is to be proclaimed at the end of every forty-
nine years in order that the freedom acquired
through the Exodus might be rediscovered by all
Israelites, and that the growing tendency toward the
concentration of rural properties in the hands of a
few might be restricted or halted (Leviticus 25:8-17).

Walking in these statutes, observing these commandments: these were indeed considered to be "the things
that make for peace."

The triple threat: famine, pestilence and the sword

The biblical triple threat to agrarian productivity and communal life was famine, sickness and war. This combination is still the very real experience of the third-world peoples who constitute approximately two-thirds of the world's population.

If obedience to God's commandments brings down Yahweh's blessing of agrarian productivity and security, failure to harken to God's *torah* will result in the reversal of the blessing on the land that was promised in Leviticus 26:3-6. The second part of chapter 26 lists the corresponding curses:[*]

"But if you will not hearken to me, and will not do all these commandments...I will appoint over you sudden terror, consumption, and fever that waste the eyes and cause life to pine away....

...and I will make your heavens like iron and your earth like brass; and your strength shall be spent in vain, for your land shall not yield its increase, and the trees of the land shall not yield their fruit.

And I will bring a sword upon you, that shall execute vengeance for the covenant; and if you gather within your cities I will send pestilence among you, and you shall be delivered into the hand of the enemy."
                                          Leviticus 26:14-16, 19-20, 25

The blessings and the curses that form the concluding chapter of the collection of legislation known as the Holiness Code, as well as the concluding selections of other legal texts in the Bible and in other manuscripts of the ancient Near East, are indicative of the aspirations of agrarian peoples and the precarious conditions of their lives.

---

[*] Leviticus 26 represents a collection of blessings and curses similar to the closing sections of major legal texts of the ancient Near East. Other biblical examples include Deuteronomy 28; Exodus 23:25ff; Joshua 24:26. This pattern is also used in Luke 6:20-26 for the "blessings and woes," the Lucan version of the Beatitudes.

In an industrializing agrarian society like that of the Philippines, monsoon flooding, devastating typhoons, prolonged drought and the escalation of militarization often destroy millions of pesos worth of rice and corn crops, and cause the dislocation of hundreds of thousands of rural people from the land that sustains them. It is becoming increasingly clear that even so-called "natural disasters" are closely linked with national and international policies of plunder which, if allowed to continue unchecked, threaten the security and survival of the entire world population.

In an article in *Third World Affairs,* Philip O'Keefe and others point out that

> Poverty is placing marginal people on marginal land. The disasters and environmental degradation that result from such processes are not Acts of God. Given current development trajectories, the poor will not inherit the earth, they will be eaten up by it.[7]

How shall we respond to such words? Shall we take them as seriously as the ruling elites of Samaria and Jerusalem took the pre-exilic prophets of doom of the eighth to the sixth centuries B.C.E.? In fact, years of preaching and warnings were to fall on deaf ears; sluggish hearts were resistant to conversion. As the nation plunged toward destruction, Isaiah understood that it had to be. Nothing less than total destruction would bring these people to their senses.

What was unavoidable for the agrarian cultivators of the ancient world, i.e., famine, pestilence and the sword of war, is today avoidable. That is to say, the world has the capability of feeding its population; of eliminating or vastly reducing the debilitating diseases endemic to third-world populations; of changing policies of plunder that cause irreparable destruction to the environment; of making decisions that would re-allocate the billions of dollars spent annually on arms to projects geared to genuine development.

As we enter on the eve of the twenty-first century we are called, as our ancestors in the faith were called, to "do the things that make for peace."

But why must the just suffer?

The "blessings and curses" theology contained in
Leviticus 26 apportions the blessing of shalom to those
who walk in Yahweh's statutes, observe God's
commands and do them; the curse of "unshalom" (the
triple threat of famine, pestilence and the sword) is
on those who fail to hearken to Yahweh's *torah*. But
the experience of Israelites at the bottom of the social
ladder was that the actual apportionment of blessings
and curses did not fall into such an easy framework.
In this connection, the Israelite who wrote Psalm 73
records a personal struggle to come to grips with
feelings of resentment and bitterness toward those
rich and powerful of the governing class who "always
at ease, . . . increase in riches" (vs. 12). Against the
parrot-like repetition of the religious truism, "truly God
is good to the upright" (vs. 1), the poet asserts a
contrasting doubt: "But as for me, my feet had almost
stumbled . . . when I saw the prosperity (shalom) of
the wicked" (vss. 2-3).[8]

Similar protests against social arrangements in which
the wicked prosper and the just are impoverished are
found in the words of Jeremiah, as well as in the
magnificent poetic pathos of the Book of Job. Jeremiah
complains,

> Righteous art thou, O Lord, when I complain to thee;
>   yet I would plead my case before thee.
> Why does the way of the wicked prosper?
> Why do all who are treacherous thrive? (12:1)

This complaint is echoed with even greater poi-
gnancy when the poet of Job cries out:

> Why do the wicked live,
>   reach old age, and grow mighty in power?
> Their children are established in their presence,
>   and their offspring before their eyes.
> Their houses are safe (shalom) from fear,
>   and no rod of God is upon them.
> Their bull breeds without fail;

> their cow calves, and does not cast her calf.
> They send forth their little ones like a flock,
>   and their children dance.
> They sing to the tambourine and the lyre,
>   and rejoice to the sound of the pipe.
> They spend their days in prosperity,
>   and in peace they go down to Sheol. (21:7-13)

> One dies in full prosperity,
>   being wholly at ease and secure,
> his body full of fat
>   and the marrow of his bones moist.
> Another dies in bitterness of soul,
>   never having tasted of good. (vss. 23-25)

As the theologian Walter Brueggemann has demonstrated, the question of why "the wicked prosper" (Jeremiah 12:1), "reach old age and grow mighty in power" (Job 21:7) arises out of an understanding that particular deeds bring certain consequences, such as we find in the blessings and curses of Leviticus, chapter 26. "The case is brought before Yahweh because he is the guarantor that certain deeds yield certain consequences, and certain consequences do or do not follow from certain deeds."[9] The question is not speculative, but grows out of concrete experiences of social practice. Not only do the wicked prosper but "they take root, they grow, they bear fruit," (Jeremiah 12:2)—visible results that make clear exactly for whom the social system functions.

If we ask the question, "why are the wicked well off?" with an informed social realism, we will find the answer: "it is because the networks of social processes which govern access and power are inclined and arranged that way."[10] While such arrangements are not divinely decreed or sanctioned, those who benefit most from the rewards of the social system frequently use religion and religious language for their legitimation.

The questions of Jeremiah and Job call us to a searching analysis and transformation of social structures and social arrangements from which a large majority of the global population are still excluded. The

just will continue to suffer until the inequities of unjust
social structures are seriously and effectively addressed.
Of the things that make for genuine and lasting peace,
social justice is central.

Justice and shalom will embrace

Frequently, the Hebrew Bible links shalom and justice
(in Hebrew, *tsedeq* or *tsedeqah*). We have seen that the
Hebrew shalom means much more than what is
indicated by the English word "peace," It often refers
to very material realities such as health (Genesis 29:6;
43:27; 2 Samuel 18:29; 20:9), prosperity (Psalm 73:3), and
agrarian productivity (Psalm 72:3, etc.). In Psalm 85,
which seems to have been a prayer for rain in the face
of prolonged drought,[11] shalom as agrarian productivity
is linked to justice.*

As a community cannot exist without water, neither
can a society continue long to survive without justice.
There is evidence that *tsedeq* was, in ancient Semitic
religion, the name of a god who became associated
with rain. Since the root of the word *tsedeq* implies "that
which is proper,"[12] it is not difficult to see how it could
be associated with a "proper" rain, i.e., a rain that comes
in its season and is not too light or too heavy—in other
words, just right! The verses read as follows:

> Yahweh indeed has promised well-being (shalom)
>   to the devoted ones of his people,
>   to those who again confide in him.

> Truly near is his prosperity
>   to those who fear him;
> Indeed his glory dwells in our land.

> Kindness (*hesed*) and fidelity (*'emeth*) will meet,
>   justice (*tsedeq*) and well-being (shalom) embrace;
> Fidelity shall sprout from the earth,
>   and justice lean down from heaven.

> With a crash will Yahweh give his rain,
>   and our land will give its produce.

* See also Psalm 72:3.

Justice will march before him,
     beauty will indeed tread in his steps. (Psalm 85:12-
14* [RSV 8-13])

We see here the personification of four attributes as
if they are attendants who cooperate with God in the
production of the needed rain. These four attributes
are kindness (*hesed*), fidelity (*'emeth*), justice (*tsedeq*) and
well-being (*shalom*).† The image connoted by fidelity
sprouting from the earth and justice leaning or coming
down from heaven pictures the earth's fruitful response
to timely rain. There is an implied interaction, with
Yahweh doing Yahweh's part and the land cooperating
by giving forth its produce.

The same connection between rain and well-being
seems to lie behind the material in Isaiah 32-33, a
collection of prophecies concerning a coming righteous
ruler. The entire collection expresses a longing and hope
for a socio-political situation characterized by justice
and right, such that each ruler

...will be like a hiding place from the wind,
   a covert from the tempest,
like streams of water in a dry place,
   like the shade of a great rock in a weary land. (32:2)

Here, a socio-political situation of justice and right
is described metaphorically in terms of refreshment in
the desert heat—a hiding place, a covert (shelter),
streams of water and the shade of a great rock.

As the chapter continues, the refreshment of socio-
political justice and right is expected to affect the
community, and as a result:

...the eyes of those who see will not be closed,
   and the ears of those who hear will hearken.
The mind of the rash will have good judgment,
   and the tongue of the stammerers will speak readily
   and distinctly.

---

* As translated by M. Dahood. See Endnote No. 11.
† Also translated by M. Dahood. We include the Hebrew words in
parentheses because the semantic richness of these terms defies adequate
rendering in any modern language.

The fool will no more be called noble,
    nor the knave said to be honorable. (32:3-5)

The chapter ends with a vision of shalom, again utilizing agrarian imagery:

Then justice will dwell in the wilderness,
    and righteousness abide in the fruitful field.
And the effect of righteousness will be peace,
    quietness and trust forever. (32:16-17)

Verses 16-17 seem to have been attached by a later editor to an earlier prophetic oracle,[13] which refers to the coming siege by the Babylonian troops that would render Jerusalem and the surrounding Judean countryside a deserted wilderness.

For the palace will be forsaken,
    the populous city deserted;
the hill and the watchtower will become dens for ever,
    a joy of wild asses, a pasture of flocks;
until the spirit is poured upon us
    from on high,
and the wilderness becomes a fruitful field,
    and the fruitful field is deemed a forest. (32:14-15)

The key here is the firm hope that the eternally ravaged and deserted city, fated to be the habitation of wild asses and domesticated flocks forever, might indeed become once again a cultivated orchard, a luxuriant forest when "the spirit is poured upon us from on high."

It was, as the prophet Isaiah makes clear, the rampant injustice and complacency of the ruling elite (cf. Isaiah 32:9-13; 33:1; and also 1:21-22; 3:13-15; 5:1-7; 5:8-24; 10:1-4, etc.) that made Judah and Jerusalem vulnerable to Babylonian defeat. They had not known "the things that make for peace." The transformation of Judah and Jerusalem would require, however, "a spirit from on high," that is, a spirit the opposite of that spirit of injustice that had led Jerusalem and its surrounding countryside to destruction.

Justice like the rain

The association of *tsedeq* (justice) and shalom in terms
of agrarian productivity, where *tsedeq* refers to the rain
that causes the land to give forth its produce, recalls
the prophet Amos's association of justice with living
waters and an "ever-flowing stream" (Amos 5:24). In
a rainfall-dependent economy like that of Palestine,
agricultural activity has to be located near small rivers
or streams and requires the capability of storing water
in lime-slaked, or sealed, cisterns. The first villages and
urban settlements in the ancient Near East were located
in the vicinity of available water.*
    How essential is justice to a community! In a critique
of the flurry of cultic activity in northern Israel during
the prosperous reign of Jeroboam II, the prophet Amos
utters the condemnation of God against the cult:

"I hate, I despise your feasts,
    and I take no delight in your solemn assemblies.
Even though you offer me your burnt offerings
    and cereal offerings,
I will not accept them,
    and the peace offerings of your fatted beasts
I will not look upon.

Take away from me the noise of your songs;
    to the melody of your harps I will not listen.

But let justice roll down like waters,
    and righteousness like an ever-flowing stream. (5:21-
24)

To repeat, if it is true that a village or urban center
cannot exist without a water supply, it is equally true
that a society cannot continue to exist without justice.
If the "just right" rains make it possible for the hillsides
to produce prosperity (shalom; Psalm 72:3), likewise,
the practice of justice within a social order makes it
possible for that society to survive. Shortsightedness

---

* Ancient Jericho (*ca.* 7000 B.C.E.) is an example. Jericho is one of the earliest
known urban settlements in the ancient Near East.

that postpones the doing of social justice is ultimately responsible for the violence that is sure to come: "...you who put far away the evil day, and bring near the seat of violence..." (Amos 6:3).

But Amos announces that northern Israel will not survive because the ruling elite of Samaria, the capital city, has "turned justice into a poisonous plant." Just as in the time of grave famine peasants are often driven to eat inedible plants, which results in death (cf. 2 Kings 4:38-41), so also when there is a famine of justice, the oppressed suffer at the hands of corrupt judges. It is an incredible paradox for the prophet that those charged with the responsibility for the doing of justice should do its opposite. In a pair of rhetorical questions Amos poses his dilemma:

Do horses run on craggy cliffs?
Does one plow the sea with oxen?
Well, you have turned judgment into a poisonous plant
and the fruit of justice into wormwood. (6:12)[14]

The implication is that horses know instinctively to run on level ground, not on craggy cliffs; and farmers have enough sense to plow a field and not the sea. But those with responsibility for assuring justice have perverted it so that instead of rolling "down like waters and...like an ever-flowing stream" (Amos 5:24), their "justice" has become like the juice of a poisonous plant which kills. Indeed, they prefer "reign" to rain!* Because of the poison present in the social system of eighth-century Israel, Amos prophesies its death:

Hear this word which I raise over you in lamentation:
"The virgin Israel has fallen down—
no more to rise.
She is left abandoned on the ground—
no one to raise her." (5:1-2)[15]

_____
* I owe this pun on "reign" and "rain" to Cindy O'Donnell, Maryknoll lay missioner in the Philippines.

They shall rebuild: the promise of the possibility of restoration

The eighth century B.C.E. prophet Amos seems to have had no good word for the ruling elite of Israel's agrarian society: "Woe to those who are at ease in Zion" (6:1). The ruling elite are, in the words of Robert Coote, "the secure, the strong, the well-to-do, the well-housed and well-fed, the authorities, the holders of power and privilege."[16] But two centuries later, toward the end of the Babylonian exile, an editor seems to have put the Amos material together in a collection to which was appended a promise of restoration or restitution.[17]

The promise of restoration after the devastation of the Babylonian destruction and dislocation is likewise couched in terms of the blessing of agricultural prosperity, such that the abundance will span the dry season, which lasts from the time of the last spring rain at harvest time to the first rain of the planting season in the fall:

"The days are coming"—oracle of Yahweh—
"when plowman will come together with the reaper
    and the treader of grapes with the sower of seed
and the mountains shall drip sweet wine
and all the hills shall melt with it
and I shall return the captivity of my people Israel
    and they shall rebuild the desolated cities and
        dwell in them

and plant vineyards and drink their wine
    and make orchards and eat their fruit
and when I plant them on their land, they shall
    never again be pulled up from their ground,
    which I have given them"
—says Yahweh your God. (Amos 9:13-15)*

It is curious that the oracle of Amos 9:13-15 speaks of rebuilding "the ruined *cities*" (italics supplied), and

---

* Robert Coote's translation. See similar passages in Isaiah 9:2-11:1-9; Micah 4:1-4; 5:2-4.

not *the* city (i.e., Jerusalem). The pre-exilic capital cities of Samaria and Jerusalem were symbols of centralized control, exaction of tribute and other oppressive measures, and as such were the focus of scathing prophetic judgment:

> What is the transgression of Jacob?
> Is it not Samaria?
> And what is the sin of the house of Judah?
> Is it not Jerusalem?

> Therefore I will make Samaria a heap in the open
>   country,
> a place for planting vineyards;
> and I will pour down her stones into the valley
> and uncover her foundations. (Micah 1:5c-6)

> Hear this, you heads of the house of Jacob. . . .
> who abhor justice and pervert all equity,
> who build Zion with blood
> and Jerusalem with wrong.

> Therefore, because of you
> Zion shall be plowed as a field;
> Jerusalem shall become a heap of ruins,
> and the mountain of the house a wooded height.
> (Micah 3:9, 12)

The poet of Amos 9:13-15 looks beyond *the* city, where the regime and its bureaucrats resided, to *cities* inhabited by those who could cultivate their own vineyards and gardens and who would actually "eat their fruit" themselves. The vision is one of a community enjoying the fruits of its labor, not as in the past, when the products of agricultural work flowed into the hands of the centralized leadership in the capital city, and when independent rural cultivators were reduced to the status of impoverished peasants.[18]

Biblical moments of crisis—and our crisis

This vision of shalom coming at the close of the Babylonian exile remains, however, just that: a vision. The story of the Israelites is a story of a people who spent a relatively short time on the stage of ancient history before meeting with destruction, deportation and dislocation at the hands of more powerful ancient empires, that is, the Assyrians and the neo-Babylonians. The assessment of the historian (or historians) responsible for the great complex of prophetic history contained in the Books of Joshua, Judges, Samuel and Kings, was that "this was so, because the people of Israel had sinned against the Lord their God,who had brought them up out of the land of Egypt..." (2 Kings 17:7a).

The Babylonian exile (589-586 B.C.E.) was only one phase of a larger dispersion, which began with the Assyrian invasion of northern Israel in 722 and accelerated during the Persian (539-332 B.C.E.) and Hellenistic (332-198 B.C.E.) periods. Jews, who retained Jerusalem as their religious and cultural center, spread broadly (the Dispersion) across the ancient world and were subject to imperial rule both in Palestine and elsewhere. A brief period of self-rule followed the civil war that broke out against the Syrian Hellenists who controlled Palestine in 167 B.C.E. This brief period of independence was brought to an end, however, by the Roman general Pompey in 63 B.C.E.[19]

Palestine had been under Roman rule for approximately ninety years when Jesus began his ministry in the towns and villages of the Galilean countryside. The life of the rural population was probably not any better during that time than it had been under the Israelite and Judean kings. This observation is supported by the fact that the Jewish peasantry at the time of Jesus produced a number of popular prophetic and messianic movements, along with banditry.[20] Eventually, elements of the Jewish population led a revolt against Rome (66-70 C.E.) which was crushed by the Romans, resulting in the destruction of the Temple and Jerusalem.

It is this impending destruction that prompts Jesus to weep over the city. Like the "envoys of peace" who wept bitterly (Isaiah 33:7) when they beheld the ravaged Judean countryside and the devastated city of

Jerusalem—a testimony to the savage might of
Nebuchadnezzer's imperial forces—Jesus weeps for a
city that seems fated for destruction. Jerusalem, the
foundation (*Jeru*) of peace and prosperity (*shalom*), is
judged for its failure to recognize and understand peace.
More specifically, Jerusalem is judged for its failure to
recognize its opportune moment, its *kairos* (Luke 19:41-
44).

Many would describe the situation of our world today
as one of grave crisis: a crisis of violence, of misery,
of social injustice and repression, and of environmental
degradation and the threat of local breakdown of the
ecological balance.[21] In Chinese languages, the
pictographic character for "crisis" contains the notions
of both "danger" and "opportunity." The global crisis
we have spoken about is a danger and a threat to all
humanity (as well as to the global ecosystem), although
it manifests itself more sharply in third-world settings
like the Philippines. But it is also an opportunity and
a challenge, especially for those of us who have
benefited from a global system of inequitable social
arrangements that has its roots in the great agrarian
social revolution of five to six thousand years ago in
the ancient Near East. It was at this time that the
prophets of Israel first recognized that there was
something in "civilization" (symbolized for the
prophets by the capital cities of Samaria and Jerusalem)
that was self-destructive. Thus they linked the failure
of the ruling class to walk in the commandments of
Yahweh to the impending destruction of the capital
cities of Samaria, in the north, and Jerusalem, in the
south. For, "the way of peace they know not and there
is no justice in their paths" (Isaiah 59:8).

As did the ancient prophets of Israel, contemporary
social scientists warn us that rich countries' pursuit
of unlimited growth will result in basic and irreversible
damage to the global ecosystem and lead ultimately
to the destruction of humanity itself. As more and more
peoples of the third world enter the struggle to obtain
their share of the world's resources, repression will
increase. The finiteness of nature simply will not allow

the estimated five billion people of the world to share equitably in the world's wealth while at the same time maintaining the rich countries' prevailing patterns of over-consumption and pollution. As a consequence, levels of happiness, justice and freedom will most certainly decline for the world as a whole in the coming decades.[22]

The history of human societies, however, demonstrates a capacity for considerable self-transcendence. If we are to be able to confront the grave problems that face us, we must act more decisively *today*. The dimensions of the crisis very briefly delineated here offer a challenge to our God-given capacity for self-transcendence. There is still time for human intervention to reverse the trends that threaten global destruction—the ultimate peacelessness. We are called, each one of us and all of us together, to learn and do "the things that make for peace."

NOTES

1. Laszio, Ervin, "Global Problems: Obstacles to Peace," in *World Encyclopedia of Peace*. Eds. Linus Pauling, Ervin Laszio and Hohn Youl Yoo (New York: Pergamon, 1986), pp 381-384

2. Galtung, Johan, *The True Worlds: A Transnational Approach* (New York: Free Press, 1980), pp. 1-39.

3. See Ricoeur, Paul, "Creativity in Language," *Philosophy Today* 17: pp. 97-111 (1973). As Ricoeur explains, words function as meaningful entities only within the framework of the sentence. Because words in natural languages have the remarkable feature of having more than one meaning, their meaning is dependent on context. Even the simplest message conveyed by the means of natural language has to be interpreted, because, (1) words are open to more than one meaning, and (2) words take their actual meaning from their connection with a particular context and audience, and against the background of a particular situation.

4. This loss by conquest began with neo-Babylonia, was followed by Persia, the Greeks and Rome. Dates given are 586-63 B.C.E., though the date 63 B.C.E. is arbitrary, being the date of the beginning of Roman rule over Palestine, a date that coincides more or less with the concluding books of the Hebrew Bible. The period was broken by a brief interval after the Maccabean Revolt when the Israelites experienced self-rule, approximately 167-163 B.C.E. See Chaney, Marvin L., "Ancient

Palestinian Peasant Movements and the Formation of
Premonarchic Israel," pp. 39-90 in *Palestine in Transition*. ed.
D.N. Freedman and D.F. Graf (Sheffield: Almond, 1983); and
"Systemic Study of the Israelite Monarchy," *Semeia* 37:53-76
(1986). Also see Gottwald, Norman K., "Israel, Social and
Economic Development of," pp. 465-68 in the *Interpreter's
Dictionary of the Bible, Supplementary Volume*, ed. K. Crim
(Nashville: Abingdon, 1976); *The Tribes of Yahweh: A Sociology
of the Religion of Liberated Israel, 1250-1050 B.C.E.*, (Maryknoll:
Orbis, 1979); and "The Participation of Free Agrarians in the
Introduction of Monarchy to Ancient Israel: An Application
of H.A. Landsberger's Framework for the Analysis of Peasant
Movements," *Semeia* 37:77-106 (1986).

5. And more recently, attention has been paid to the tensive
character of living language, especially of poetic language
which, according to Philip Wheelwright (in *Metaphor and
Reality* [Bloomington: Indiana University, 1962]) "partly creates
and partly discloses certain hitherto unknown, unguessed
aspects of What Is." The starting point for the new approach
is the insight that words alone cannot be metaphors, only
a complete statement can be metaphorical. Metaphor is the
unity of the tension between two poles which are designated
by the word-pair *vehicle* and *tenor*. The imagery of concrete
situation described is the vehicle, and the ulterior significance
that this concrete situation suggests to the responsive
imagination is termed the tenor. The power of metaphor, as
Ricoeur notes (Endnote 3, p. 127), is the capacity "to break
through previous categorization and to establish new logical
boundaries on the ruins of the preceding ones." Ordinary
language aims at improving communication through the
limiting or reduction of ambiguity. But speech that employs
metaphor has the extraordinary power of redescribing reality.
"Metaphor not only shatters the previous structures of our
language, but also the previous structures of what we call
reality" (Ricoeur, p. 111). As we observe in the article, the
use of shalom in the poetic material of the Scripture is often
metaphorical.

6. Brueggemann, Walter, "'Vine and Fig Tree': A Case Study in
Imagination and Criticism." *CBQ* 43:188-204, (1981).

7. Ibid, p. 243.

8. Graham, Helen R., "Towards Total Transformation: Reflections
on Psalm 73, *Witness* 2:74-78.

9. Brueggemann, Walter, "Theodicy in a Social Dimension," *JSOT*
33: 3-25, (1985), p. 11.

10. Ibid, p. 13.

11. Dahood, Michael, *The Psalms, Vol. 2*, Anchor Bible Series (New
York: Doubleday and Co., 1968), p. 289.

12. Ibid, p. 290.

13. Moriarty, Frederick L., "Isaiah 1-39," pp 265-282 in *The Jerome Biblical Commentary*, eds. Raymond E. Brown, Joseph A. Fitzmyer and Roland E. Murphy (New Jersey: Prentice Hall, 1968).
14. Translation by Robert B. Coote, *Amos Among the Prophets: Composition and Theology* (Philadelphia: Fortress, 1983).
15. Ibid.
16. Ibid, p. 16.
17. See the first chapter of Coote's monograph (Note 16) for an explanation of the stages of composition that most likely lie behind the final text of the Book of Amos. A more complex six-stage theory is presented by Hans W. Wolff in his commentary on the Book of Amos, *Joel and Amos* (Philadelphia: Fortress Press, 1977).
18. There has been much debate about the problem of defining "peasant." Norman Gottwald employs Landsberger's framework in his premise that the vast majority of Israelites became peasants in Landsberger's sense of "rural cultivators of low economic and political status," as measured by the degree of their control over critical "resource inputs," over "transformation processes," and over the benefits of "output," in his 1986 *Semeia* article (p. 78ff., *op. cit.*).
19. Gottwald, Norman K., *The Hebrew Bible: A Socio-Literary Introduction*. (Philadelphia: Fortress, 1985), pp. 420-456.
20. Horsely, Richard A., "The Sicarii: Ancient Jewish 'Terrorists,'" *The Journal of Religion* 59:435-458 (1979); "Ancient Jewish Banditry and the Revolt Against Rome, A.D. 66-70," *CBQ* 43:409-432 (1981); "Popular Messianic Movements Around the Time of Jesus," *CBQ* 46:471-495 (1984); "'Like One of the Prophets of Old': Two Types of Popular Prophets at the Time of Jesus," *CBQ* 47:435-463 (1985); and "Menahem in Jerusalem: A Brief Messianic Episode Among the Sicarrii—Not 'Zealot Messianism,'" *Nov. Test* 27:334-348 (1985).
21. Galtung, Johan, *The True Worlds, op. cit.*, pp. 1-39.
22. Lenski G. and Lenski J., *Human Societies: An Introduction to Macrosociology*, 4th ed. (New York: McGraw Hill, 1982), pp. 407-442.

Editors' Note

A growing body of Filipino Christians, both Catholic and Protestant, insist that doing theology is not a task reserved for scholars, academics and professional clergy, but one given to the whole people of God, to every faithful follower of Christ.

This tradition holds that the most authentic expressions of theology are not necessarily found in books or learned papers, but may be seen and experienced in the reflections, poetry, songs and stories of ordinary people.

Theological reflection is not primarily an intellectual exercise, they say: it does not begin with "thinking," but actually begins with faith as expressed in an act of commitment. It is not just listening and under- standing and articulating verbally or in writing. Rather, doing theology is a way of life.

The renewed interest in carefully studying the Bible in small groups has led many to the conviction that present conditions of injustice are contrary to God's will, and that Christians not only have permission but are called to struggle for redemptive change.

The chapter that follows should help us to better understand such an approach to theology, and to appreciate why some people, particularly those who feel threatened by political and economic change, are so anxious about the dynamic nature of some of the theologies emerging from the third world.

WHEN DID WE SEE YOU, LORD?

Rebecca C. Asedillo

"Jesus' death has set an example for all Christians. He suffered and died not for himself, but for others. Therefore I must carry on because in him, in what he did, we find hope." The speaker, a woman in a small reflection group, went on: "His resurrection, on the other hand, means that there will be victory in the end, after all our sacrifices."

The thoughts are simple, uncomplicated. But when Maria spoke about "making sacrifices," she also meant the literal possibility of following Jesus' example: of being arrested on false charges, being tortured and summarily executed. She herself had been apprehended, threatened and interrogated by a paramilitary group because they suspected her of being a subversive.

Other Christian lay leaders have suffered a worse fate. Nestor Gallines was hacked, shot and beheaded by the right-wing vigilante group called Alsa Masa. Tranquilino Amasola and Agustin Lozo were also hacked to death by the Tadtads, another paramilitary group. All were active leaders in their parishes and in Basic Christian Communities.

A squatter community in Davao City had just successfully participated in putting up human barricades to prevent a big company from ejecting them from their land. One day they held a prayer rally on a hilltop and there reflected on their experience. They were sharing that Bible passage which says, "And God

gave his people land flowing with milk and honey,"
when an old woman stood up and said, "We have
listened to the word of God that says God will give
his people land. But here we are, being threatened with
ejection. Where is God now, if God is alive?" There
was silence. All of a sudden, in a flash of insight, the
same woman said, "I know. At this moment, I see God
in our midst as we gather together to stand for our
rights and prevent our homes and our lives from being
demolished."

Members of another Bible reflection group on a sugar
plantation on the hunger-ravaged island of Negros were
talking about the times when they felt the presence
of Christ. A sugar worker (these are among those most
exploited in the Philippines) said, "I saw a mother with
three starving children in the cane field. The children
were crying because they were hungry, but the mother
had nothing to feed them. So, with her bare hands,
she started to squeeze the juice out of the sugar cane
and gave it to her children. I discovered Christ in that
life-giving act."

The poor are able to see the face of the liberating
Christ even in the most dehumanizing situations.[1]

A theology of people in struggle

The Philippines is a land of deepening economic and
political crisis and intensifying militarization. But
despite these conditions, Christian communities have
struggled and are struggling to live out their commitment to the gospel and its message of justice and
liberation for the oppressed. In the process, a "theology
of struggle," or a "theology of people in struggle" has
arisen. It is not an elaborate theology articulated by
scholars in books, but one that comes from ordinary
people reflecting upon the Bible in light of their day-
to-day experience.

A theology of the poor

At least seventy percent of Filipinos are very poor.
By "poor," we mean that they are unable to obtain

three square meals a day, or adequate nutrition; that
they do not have access to basic health care and
education, to adequate housing or an adequate income.
Neither do they have access to land, which is needed
in order to survive in an agricultural economy.

Since theology deals with the interaction between
God and humans, it is important to note that the
"human sphere" is experienced in very concrete,
historical terms and perceived in ways that are
determined by the conditions of a person's class, race
and sex. What the theology of struggle has done and
is doing is to take the life situation and questions of
the poor as a central base for doing theology, or
reflecting on the meaning of God, salvation, the reign
of God and other dimensions of faith.

Why the poor? One could say that the poor are
central because in the Philippines they constitute the
majority—a majority that is, however, controlled and
dominated by a small social and economic elite. One
could also say that from the perspective of Christian
faith, God has taken the side of the poor and the
oppressed. This is established in the biblical prophetic
tradition and in the gospel. Therefore it is not only
legitimate to assume but is an inherent truth from the
standpoint of Christian faith, that God has a central
interest in the poor and in how they can be saved
or liberated.

To understand the "theology of struggle," middle-
class Christians from North America or from the West
have to take a jump into a world defined by the need
to survive physically—to survive hunger and survive
the exigencies of a militarized society. Stories sometimes
help to drive this point home. For example, a fact-
finding mission to investigate human rights abuses
came upon a remote barrio in the southern Philippines
where villagers related the terror of having their houses
strafed and family members killed and wounded. At
one point, a member of the mission asked, "Why don't
you people move? Why do you insist on living here?"
The answer was, "If we stay, we have one enemy: the

bullet. If we move, we have three: breakfast, lunch and dinner!"

For many people in the Philippines, the options are that limited. Some have moved, or have been forced to move. From January to December 1987, 18,786 Filipino families were forced to evacuate their homes and live in evacuation centers or with relatives as a result of military operations in their towns and villages. Others decided to stay put, to live from day to day on whatever they could garner from the land, and to face the bullet.

In a theology of struggle, historical circumstances such as those described above cannot be divorced from the question of God and faith. To the poor, poverty and oppression are not mere economic and political issues, but theological questions as well. In the midst of their suffering and want, they ask, "Why, God? If you are our parent and we are your children, why is it that the landlord inherits the land while the peasants only inherit debts?"

Edicio de la Torre, a former priest who spent nine years in jail during the Marcos regime, likes to tell stories about his experiences with farmers and peasants. One day, he says, he came upon a group of peasants at a village store. "Tell me," he said, what is it that the church should do? What should we preach?" To which a peasant leader replied: "You priests are always telling us this: don't smoke, don't drink, don't gamble, don't sleep with any woman who is not your wife. But you know, you are only addressing the periphery of my life: my weekends and my nightlife. Every day, from sunup to sundown, I'm in the field, plowing. What do you have to say to that? If I harvest fifty bags of rice instead of twenty-five, does that make me a better Christian?" De la Torre went away feeling perplexed, but as he confessed, it led him to search for a more relevant Christian theology for Filipinos.

A theology based on a critical look at society

A group of laborers at the huge Saint Ines Melalia Lumber & Plywood Company were talking about the biblical concept of justice. "Every week we watch ships roll out of the harbor, bound for the United States, Europe and Japan, filled with the lumber and plywood that we sweat to make. Meanwhile, our pay is not even enough to feed our families decently. What is more, soon these big companies will have taken all the timber, and what will be left in the forests for our children? Where is God's justice?" they asked.

Lina, the wife of a laborer, said: "Before, I didn't wonder about the reasons for the suffering of so many because we were able to eat three times a day and move around our neighborhood and along the roads without fear. And before, I used to believe that the poverty of the people was the way things were meant to be, the will of God. But now that I have learned more I understand that this hardship that we suffer is not the will of God, but rather that of men who are greedy for riches and power. Our situation is so hard these days that we almost cannot eat three times a day because prices are so high. And there is no certainty in our lives and no future for our children. So it is right that the people will act now, especially the women. . . . "[2]

This theology of struggle is one articulated by people who are making a critical analysis of their social situation, those who "suffer, and therefore struggle," according to de la Torre's categorization. Their view of reality is that of people at the bottom of the social and economic spectrum who are aware of their situation and seek to change it.

Oftentimes, the heightening of people's critical awareness occurs in the context of Bible study sharing. A Protestant Bible study group studying the "reign of God" was using Luke 3:3-14 as their text. Verses 9-14 of this passage state:

"Even now the axe is laid to the root of the trees; every tree therefore that does not bear good fruit is cut down and thrown into the fire."
And the multitudes asked him [John the Baptist], "What then shall we do?" And he answered them,

"He who has two coats, let him share with him who has none; and he who has food, let him do likewise." Tax collectors also came to be baptized and said to him, "Teacher, what shall we do?" And he said to them, "Collect no more than is appointed you." Soldiers also asked him, "And we, what shall we do?" And he said to them, "Rob no one by violence or by false accusation, and be content with your wages."

The sharing went something like this:

"Sometimes the soldiers are not satisfied, not content."

"Especially the highway patrol. . . ."

"Now it is clear to us that this should not happen."

"That is a sin. We must be sorry. Because if we're not, then the axe awaits us."

"For every period, God gives a sign. What is the content, what is the scope of this? The first is repentance for sins. The second has to do with the economy. What we are discussing here is entirely about our life today, not the life to come. When we speak of God's kingdom, we speak of our day-to-day life: our clothes, food, taxes—things economic. About the soldier, we speak of things that deal with morals and politics."

"I noticed something . . . the tax on our land is rather high."

"That is true. One thousand pesos has gone into the taxman's pocket." (Pointing to figures on the chalkboard stating that public officials charge exorbitant taxes and that the system for collecting taxes is defective. Laughter.)

"It can't be just one thousand pesos."

"How many of you are victims of this?"

"Aside from us, there's the relative of Vivian. And especially the relative of Lukas because he is now suffering from depression."

"Why did you not complain?"

"We were victims of high taxes."

"There were many victims . . ."

". . . How can we be saved?"

(About the soldiers) "How can soldiers be content with their salaries?"

"A policeman receives 855 pesos [$43 U.S.] How can he live reasonably without extorting money? The very law that sets salaries is severe. So where is justice? We cannot blame them. They are also victims of the system. . . ."

"What shall we do?"

"Get the axe ready!"

"How many times has the axe been swung? It has not simply been ready. It has nearly cut the tree down."

". . . But how can we be saved? We have no strength."

"We are like ants. Very tiny, but working together, not alone. . . ."[3]

A theology towards transforming action

Father Carlos Abesamis, a Filipino Jesuit Bible scholar, once wrote:

We have always known in some way that good theology must lead to a good pastoral action. But somehow, our long association with Greek metaphysics has conditioned us to regard theology as abstruse speculation. Now, praxis, analysis, and faith all conspire to make us see that for theology, too, the point is not to contemplate or explain the world but to change it. And so we speak of a theology that leads to transforming action. And whereas any good theology must lead at least to individual transformation, we see that today's theology must not only do this but go beyond this and contribute to total life through societal transformation.[4]

As stated earlier, a theology of struggle is made by people in struggle—by people engaged in concrete action. This presupposes a prior commitment to the struggles of the poor and the exploited. Therefore, as in liberation theology, the matter of engaging in theological reflection becomes a secondary act; committed action precedes it.

The *action* component usually has this goal: to change
the condition that denies the "image of God," the
condition as seen in the dehumanization and deprivation of God's children among the poor and oppressed.
Oftentimes this stance poses a threat to those whose
interests and power are protected by the status quo.
Inevitably, conflict results.

A Redemptorist priest, Father Louie Hechanova,
shares the following story:

> I used to make it a point to say Mass in the *hacienda*
> (sugar plantation) run by a very close relative of
> mine. I would go there once a month and after
> Mass would remain for a while to chat with the
> people and listen to their problems. Remembering
> the course I had done at the Institute of Social
> Order (ISO), I suggested as solutions to their
> problems credit unions and cooperatives. The
> people just looked at me. "What do we put into
> the credit union? During the off-season, when
> work is slack and our earnings low, we have to
> get advances from the canteen. When milling
> starts, what we earn is deducted from our debts."
>
> I quickly saw that what I was offering were
> answers but not solutions. In any case, I tried
> playing the role of intermediary between my
> *hacendero* relative and his workers. But his constant
> reply to my suggestions was this: "Look, you don't
> understand. I am just a member of the Federation
> of Sugar Planters. Do you know what they would
> do to me if I did something different? They would
> gang up on me, and I cannot afford it.
>
> It was then that I understood what being a class
> meant. I did not learn it from Marx, nor from the
> sugar workers. I discovered the existence and
> reality of class from the way the *hacenderos* acted
> as a class to protect their interests.
>
> But to continue the story, there was a period
> when I got involved in a big mission that kept
> me on the go for several months. Returning to
> that *hacienda* after an absence of a few months,

I was struck by the way the situation of the workers had deteriorated. After a year and a half of mediatory work, nothing had changed except for the worse.

As I was saying Mass, guilt feelings rushed into me. I was so overcome that I broke down in front of the people. I could not finish the Mass. It was not from any high-sounding principle: no justice, no Eucharist. It was simply the experience of the moment, the experience of failure to do anything for them. I could not look at the people straight in the eyes. I knew then that I had to face the inevitable choice. The next time, I met my *hacendero* relative, I told him: "For over a year and a half now I have tried to act as an intermediary between you and your workers. You have not listened and you have not done anything. Please do not blame me if you are going to get labor trouble. And when it comes, please know on which side I'll be."[5]

Some charge that such thinking leads to "class struggle." It must be emphasized that people's solidarity does not aim at the victory of one class over another, or at domination, but aims at justice and participation.

Other instances of congregational or corporate action may be cited: On December 9, 1984, the Mangagoy United Church of Christ in the Philippines (UCCP) of Bislig, Surigao del Sur in Mindanao decided to forego their regular Sunday morning service to join hands with the striking workers of a paper company who were starting to get harassed by the military. They held their worship service in the middle of the picket line. In the same province, in a remote village called Salvacion, members of a small UCCP congregation braved the rain and walked seven kilometers to the Philippine Constabulary headquarters where some of their members were being detained, humming as they went along, "I Surrender All." Clearly, they were surrendering not to the military, but to the Spirit that spurred them to take this action!

A theology articulated in images, songs, poetry, liturgy

The *reflection* component of a theology of struggle takes many different forms. From traditional and popular religiosity to militant prayer vigils in the streets, it is expressed in stories, songs and indigenous liturgies.

On the "challenge of the gospel," for instance, one song goes:

Ang hamon ng Ebanghelyo para sa atin
Mahalin ang kapatid at sila'y kilalanin
Nguni't kung taos-puso ang pagserbisyo
Tatahakin na daan ay doon papuntang Kalbaryo.

Koro:

Di madali ang pagsunod kay Kristo
Maraming tinik ang daang lalakbayin mo
Mabigat ang krus na papasanin mo
At kamatayan ay siyang haharap sa iyo.

Si Kristo mismo ang nagwika at nagpaalala
Magingat baka hulihin kayo mga kasama
Hahantong kayo sa madilim na bilangguan
At doon kayo'y hahatulan ng may kapangyarihan.

Mapalad ang inuusig at pinahihirapan
Ng dahil sa kanilang pinaniniwalaan
Mapalad ang makibaka para sa katarungan
Kaligayaha'y makakamtan, pati na ang kaharian.

Translation:

The challenge of the gospel for us
Is to love our brother/sister
But when we truly serve them
We shall walk the path that leads to Calvary.

Chorus:

It isn't easy to follow Christ
The path is full of thorns
The cross you bear is heavy

And death shall confront you.

Christ himself has warned us
Be vigilant for you may be arrested
And may end up in dark prison
And be put in trial by the authorities.

Blessed are the persecuted
And those made to suffer for their belief.
Blessed are those who struggle for justice,
Happiness will be theirs, as well as the kingdom.

In the tradition of the psalmist, prayers for deliverance are expressed in such ways as this (a translation):

Lord, save us from our enemies,
from foreigners who exploit the wealth of our land,
from our own folks who oppress and deceive.
Save us from those who rule the land.

They surround us, corrupt our minds, emotions,
    and beliefs.
We see their propaganda in our newspapers.
Their voices dominate the air waves.
They are like leeches that crawl from our hair
    down to our toes.

Save us, Lord, from our enemies.
They exploit our weaknesses and
take away from us what is left of our life and
    freedom.

Save us, Lord, like you saved the Israelites.
Help us to become like Moses who will lead us
    on the path of change.[6]

Long before the theme of "God's preferential option for the poor" was ever raised, Filipino peasants had come to the conclusion that God has a special love for poor people. The following is a transcription of a dialogue among them:

"How do we know that a person has a special love for some people?" Mang Jose asks. "When that person celebrates his birthday, we can tell who his special friends are by knowing whom he has invited on that day.

"When God celebrated his first 'birthday,' whom did he invite on that day? None other than peasants, shepherds, the poor people. It is true that he also invited the educated, the kings and the rich, but not immediately for that day.

"And while God only sent a star to invite the kings and the learned, God sent a whole host of angels to invite the peasants and the shepherds." With humorous seriousness, Mang Jose concludes, "So you see, we are God's favorites.

"Moreover, when God instituted the Mass, God showed again how much God values us peasants. What are the more important elements in the celebration of the Mass? Is it the church building which engineers constructed? The chairs or the pews, perhaps? No, because we can have Mass without all these. Rather, it is the bread and the wine that become the body and blood of Christ: the bread that comes from wheat that's planted by the peasants. Without the peasants, there is no Mass. And in fact, if one has no communion with the masses, there is no meaning to the Communion at Mass.

"Finally, when he started his 'organization,' whom did he choose as his first 'leaders?'

"If I had been in God's place," Mang Jose emphasizes, "I might, perhaps, have started in Rome instead of Bethlehem; be born son of the emperor, get the senators, the politicians, the generals, and in relatively short time, 'conquer' the whole world with no more need for crucifixion.

"Instead, with all God's wisdom, God started in Galilee, a small town, and chose, as first leaders, the peasants and the fishermen. So, I say, the importance of the peasants is recognized not only before society, but in the eyes of God, too. The problem, however, is that too often the peasants themselves do not realize their own importance."

The voice of Mang Jose is emphatic: "We must now wake up to our own importance and to our dignity, and unite in saying that we can forge our own destiny."

Another peasant in the meeting objects: "If God loves us so much that we have become God's favorites, how come we are so poor and expoited? How come we suffer so much injustice? Is this God's way of showing us his love?"

In answer, Mang Jose says, "The God who loves us is Creator. But we cannot pray to God 'up there' and say, 'God Creator, you love us; we have a land problem, please create more lands!' For although God is indeed Creator, God wants us to co-create with him.

"God makes the crop to grow, but will not make it grow unless we plant it. God will not even create a single human being without the co-creative help of a man and a woman. Neither will God create a just, humane society unless we do our part and struggle for liberation from landlordism and usury and other oppressive forces."[7]

But what about middle-class Christians?

If the theology of struggle is a theology of the struggling poor, where does that leave middle-class Christians?

In a religious tradition that emphasizes reconciliation and forgiveness, the point raised earlier by the peasants becomes problematic, especially for the non-poor. Again, some peasants have a way of clarifying the issue:

One peasant was talking to his priest: "I'm fighting to get my proper share of the harvest, so I have taken my landlord to court. But when I bring him to court, I fight with him. When I fight with him, I get angry with him. And when I get angry with him, I am told, 'You're not a very good Christian, because Christians are not supposed to get angry and to fight.'

"Then I go to church and I ask what they have to say. And the Church would say, 'Do you not see, I am a mother and you are my children—the landlord is my child and the peasant is my child—and I cannot take sides.' What kind of a mother is that? When a young, weak child is being beaten by an elder child, the mother takes sides. In so doing, she does not stop from being a mother.

"I go to the bishops and the priests and ask them, 'Speak, will you side with the peasants or with the landlords?' And the bishops and the priests would say, 'Yes, perhaps we should take sides. But that is not our central vocation because we are called to reconcile, to build bridges.' Well, have you ever built bridges starting from the middle?"[8]

We must challenge here the simplistic notion that taking sides might lead to more violence, noting that solidarity movements which become "groundswells" have greater possibilities of using the democratic process to effect change.

Edicio de la Torre, speaking of the parable of the Good Samaritan, offers some interesting insights on this. He says that often we identify the Christian with the Good Samaritan, the person in the middle between the victim and the robber. Then he tells an apocryphal version of the story in which the Good Samaritan keeps coming week after week, and there is victim after victim, and he says, "This is a social problem! I'd better get around to my fellow Good Samaritans, set up a trust fund and put up a Good Samaritan Hospital."

So each victim is taken care of. The Good Samaritan counsels the robber, trying to understand him as a human being because, as the robber tells him, "I've got problems too. My children have too much money, and they're into drugs."

But one day, the Good Samaritan comes too early! The robber is still there, robbing the victim, and the victim is resisting. The Samaritan is seeing both sides in conflict, *and he wants to love*, to be involved, but how? It is easy to say, "I want to love you both. Please stop and listen to me." But if they don't listen, what do you do? Taking sides is not easy, but it is necessary.[9]

Father Louie Hechanova, quoted earlier, who himself comes from a landed family, said:

I have found most *hacenderos* (sugar plantation
owners) to be good, sincere and generous people—
taken individually. But as a class their behavior
is different. The system that protects them also
gives them the justification to oppose whatever
militates against that system. In many cases, they
do not merely represent the system, they are
actually victims of the system itself.... This
realization led me to tone down somewhat the
denunciation aspect in my preaching. I began to
realize that denouncing the injustices of the
oppressors was virtually acknowledging that the
solution was going to come from them. Whereas
I had reached the point of becoming convinced
that their liberation as an oppressor class would
come only through pressure from below. It is when
the poor themselves get liberated that a liberation
would occur among the rich.[10]

A common experience among middle-class Christians who decide to give the "option for the poor" a
try is that of feeling humbled by the example of those
they had set out to serve. For example, a nun who
worked in labor organizing narrated how, one day, a
picket line was attacked by the police, killing two of
the workers and injuring others. To defend themselves,
the workers overturned a police car and used it as a
shield. The following day, two policemen came to
retrieve their vehicle but found they could not move
it. The workers had returned to the picket line that
day and were watching the policemen. Finally, the
union leader said, "Okay, let's help. But go back at
once to the picket line." Some nuns who were indignant
over the violence that had happened the day before
were aghast, but later felt that it had been a learning
experience for them.

In a theology of struggle, the middle-class Christian
is therefore challenged, first, to be open to the cries
of the poor, to understand and respect their struggles
and then to identify with them, if possible, and to be
humble enough to learn from them.

"For those of us who are not poor," says missionary Brendan Lovett, "there is only one way towards true life, and that is what the gospel calls poverty in spirit: solidarity with the poor in their struggle. That solidarity is appropriately defined as poverty of spirit because you can't be there, truly there, unless you let go, in a significant way, of class identity and a whole set of values, of ways of thinking that take for granted as truth the world and the way things should be. This concept of solidarity with people is an extremely costly concept. You can't truthfully stand with them unless you are undergoing conversion. You have to be undergoing revolution in your mind, in your thinking, in your understanding and in your self-definition if this solidarity is to be authentic."[11]

Some of those reading the Bible with a new excitement because of the Exodus liberation theme have suggested that North American Christians might reread Exodus from the point of view of the Egyptians. It was an Egyptian who saved the baby Moses from being killed prematurely. And as a child, Christ was taken to Egypt to evade Herod.

The history of the United States includes such stories. The underground railroad helped thousands of men, women and children escape the horrors of slavery. Today, the sanctuary movement helps shelter Central Americans who have been forced out of their country by military operations or death threats.

Edicio de la Torre reflects:

> I would like to propose as the theological preparation for your politics of liberation a serious reading of Exodus from the point of view of the Egyptians! After all, why should only the Israelites be liberated? There were many Egyptians left behind, and I am sure some of those left behind were also grumbling when they had to make bricks without straw and saying, "When will we get liberated from our Pharoah?"[12]

Many American workers could identify with this passage. Farmworkers in Ohio, California and New

Jersey do the back-breaking work that few would be willing to do, for a fraction of the wage they need to support their families. Coalminers in Appalachia, who have a long and bloody history of struggle for decent working conditions and wages, continue their battles with the coal companies.[13]

Another prevalent reality in the United States today is the loss of work due to factories closing and moving to countries with lower wages. Lorraine Grey, in her excellent film, "Global Assembly Line," documents the effects of U.S. manufacturing firms closing factories in the United States in search of lower labor costs in third-world countries like Mexico and the Philippines. The governmental and economic forces that keep third-world workers in poverty are the same forces that result in the loss of jobs for American workers. Perhaps, as de la Torre suggests, Egyptian and Israelite workers have more to hold in common than to dispute.

People in the third world engaged in their liberation struggles teach their North American sisters and brothers and continually challenge them to be in solidarity with them, not in any paternalistic sort of way, but in view of the fact that the liberation of one is bound up with the liberation of the other.

Such challenge implies not only theological and spiritual preparedness. A concrete historical project and goal are absolutely essential.

NOTES

1. Sheila S. Coronel, "Who's Afraid of the Theology of Liberation," *Philippine Panorama,* 10/14/84, p. 10.
2. Christina Cobourn, "People's Theology: An Articulation of Hope in the Philippines," Mennonite Central Committee News Service, January 3, 1986
3. *Faith in Struggle, Book I,* translated by Jo Ann Maglipon. (Ecumenical Center for Development, 1985), pp. 28-30.
4. As quoted by Karl Gaspar in *Pumipiglas; Teolohiya ng Bayan.* (Socio-Pastoral Institute, 1986), p. 26.
5. Fr. Louie G. Hechanova, CSsR, "The Christ of Liberation Theology, *With Raging Hope,* SPI Series on Church and Social Transformation, Vol. 1 (Quezon City: Claretian Press, 1985).
6. *Pumipiglas, op. cit.,* pp. 25-26, 23-24. Translations by the author.

7. From *Peasant Theology*, World Student Christian Federation—Asia, 1976, pp. 21-23.
8. Edicio de la Torre, "Faith and Struggle: The Testimony of a Filipino Christian," Speech given at the Christian Conference of Asia Assembly in Bangalore, India, in May 1981 after his first release from prison. He was subsequently rearrested and imprisoned from April 1982 to February 1986.
9. Edicio de la Torre, "The Philippines: Christians and the Politics of Liberation," *Tugon*, Vol. VI, No. 3, (1986), on the theme "Theology, Politics and Struggle," 1982, p. 65. Italics added.
10. Hechanova, *op. cit.* pp. 9-10.
11. Quoted in *Pumipiglas*, p. 49.
12. From *Tugon*, Vol. VI, No. 3, *Theology, Politics and Struggle* (Quezon City: National Council of Churches in the Philippines, 1986).
13. Jim Naughton, "Matewan," *Washington Post*, (Sunday, November 29, 1987), p. F1.

MORE THAN JUSTICE

B. David Williams

As an American Christian trying to grasp the collective implications of the young rich man's question, "What must we do to be saved?" (Matthew 19:16), I find myself realizing that the biblical vision of "shalom" must not be seen merely in terms of the various conditions and elements that make for righteousness or fairness, but rather, as Helen Graham's article reminds us, it must involve systemic change that can nurture *a whole culture of peace*, indeed a "culture of wholeness." The Shalom Way is something deeply rooted in values, attitudes, habits and disciplines. While justice is surely at its heart, the Shalom Way is something alive, dynamic, creative, having its own inner life and strength:

> Steadfast love and faithfulness will meet;
>   righteousness and peace will kiss each other.
> Faithfulness will spring up from the ground,
>   and righteousness will look down from the sky.
> (Psalm 85:10-11)

Strangely enough, such a view turns us back to the centers of conflict, to our own "Jerusalems," and there we experience the Resurrection, on the other side of a cross.

So even while we would struggle for justice in concrete situations like that of the Philippines, we need to seek more than justice—we need to seek the creation and re-creation of a *culture* of justice and peace having power to overcome the cultures of violence and to deal with their wreckage. The "swords into plowshares" passages (Isaiah 2:4 and Micah 4:3) say "they shall not *learn* war any more"! When Isaiah (65:25) speaks of the wolf and the lamb feeding together, he was referring to a condition of profound conversion!

As one who yearns for economic, social and political change not only in the Philippines but in my own society as well, and in every other place, I feel at times overcome with the difficulties entailed in resisting a pervasive culture. I have come to believe that a culture of violence can increase its power over us to the extent that our very capacity to "find" our lost selves, or come to our senses, may be destroyed.

But I continue to marvel at the richness of the biblical accounts of similar struggles, and the growing tradition of struggle and hope of which we are a part. This is one reason why I consider the emerging theology of struggle presently nurtured by some Filipino Christians as one that feeds my own faith journey.

Much of what really matters to me comes together theologically and in concrete terms when I think seriously about what a true *culture* of peace might entail: how it would deal with the realities of evil and suffering; with the power of Sin; with the greater power of the Cross and the possibilities for redemption; and how it would lay claim to the incarnation of God in Christ, the creative word, sign and substance of God's practical, concrete involvement in history in response to the cries of ordinary people.

It is the faith community that must understand and act upon these things. We are called to participate in uncovering that which is "hid"; to participate in nurturing the seeds already sown which show themselves all around us in the creative and creating struggle.

How can we as North Americans adequately express our caring, our practical, active concern for the Filipino people? The present crisis challenges and judges us.

"What must we do?" This is a good American question, and there are indeed urgent things to be done. We must *do*. Yet we must go beyond doing to ask how the Philippines and some other regional crisis situations concretely reflect who we have become. Our own selfhood is at stake as well as the selfhood of Filipinos. Our own liberation is bound up with theirs.

As for doing: will we stop our insistence on military solutions for the long-standing unrest? Will we withdraw our support from the elitist elements in the Philippines, which are essentially anti-democratic?

Why did it take us so long to express our outrage and disgust at the consistent, blatant violations of human rights that occurred under Ferdinand Marcos? Why is it that the "agenda" of groups in the Philippines struggling for economic and political change so embarrasses and threatens us as a nation?

Will U.S. intervention in the Philippines become more direct? Unfortunately, history indicates that it will, and high U.S. officials have inferred that there are circumstances in which direct military intervention might be undertaken. Such a dreadful mistake would kill many, many people. The American people must not allow that to happen.

The Philippines is not "something we could lose"— it does not belong to us. Filipinos are not simple-minded people incapable of resisting "foreign" ideologies—they are a gifted people with minds and values of their own, a people who love democracy! Filipino nationalism is not a sinister force. Let us affirm with Filipinos: "Yes, it is good to love one's country, to struggle for one's selfhood."

Will Americans have the grace to leave the question of U.S. bases in the Philippines to Filipinos? If Filipinos decide not to renew the U.S.-Philippines bases agreement, will we respect that choice?*

Going to a deeper level: the current crisis is not a new question, nor is it a partisan issue. The United States' direct involvement in the Philippines has now spanned sixteen U.S. presidencies. What are the deep attitudes and values revealed here? Are we betraying

---

* The National Council of Churches in the Philippines has passed a resolution calling for the removal of the U.S. bases from the Philippines and has formally requested the National Council of the Churches of Christ in the U.S.A to support them in their action. See Appendix V.

ourselves? What is it that we need to change in ourselves? Have we spawned a self-feeding "national security culture" that will, in the end, alienate many, devour us, and take many with us? Of whom, really, are we afraid?

What prophetic call should be sounding forth from our churches concerning this, our crisis of culture? Filipino Christians, in their struggles, have so much to teach us.

With deep gratitude for the countless ties and enduring special bonds we have with the Filipino people, and in contrition for serious mistakes in the Philippines, Americans, let us LET GO!

This is how to pave the way for the renewal of a precious relationship.

As for our security: as a people of faith, we know that the God of Abraham and Sarah, Rebekah and Isaac, Rachel and Jacob is our refuge. We know that "righteousness exalteth a nation," and that it is in God we trust.

APPENDIX I

Windows of Understanding: A Glossary

We invite our readers to treat this glossary as a chapter in itself, and hope that they will find it both informative and interesting. Please note that there are more than 80 dialects in the Philippines. Languages there are a truly dynamic phenomenon. Many of the Pilipino (national language) terms are used in a number of the dialects.

Regarding pronunciation: This glossary has been prepared mainly for reading, and not for speaking! For your information, however: the Spanish words here are pronounced in the Spanish way, as are the other words, generally. Authentic pronunciation in the Philippine languages, as in most languages, is a complex matter that we won't go into here. It is said, for example, that the ancient Tagalog alphabet was composed of 3 vowels and 14 consonants (one symbol for "e" and "i"; one for "o" and "u").* You will rarely hear an "a" pronounced the way North Americans do in the words "ham" or "flat," for example, and there is rarely a long "a" as in "table." You will almost always hear "a" as in "father." The use of accents is important too, since using different accents occasionally produces serious differences in meaning.

adobo: a popular way of cooking chicken or pork using vinegar, soy sauce, garlic and black peppercorns (See Recipes, in *The Sari-Sari Store: A Philippine Scrapbook*).
amor propio: self esteem, sensitivity to personal affront.
anitos: supernatural spirits.
archipelago: a sea with many islands, or a group of many islands.

---

* Institute of National Language, *English-Tagalog Dictionary,* Manila: Bureau of Printing, Republic of the Philippines, 1960.

bahala na: means, literally, leaving things to Bathala (God), or letting things take care of themselves.

balato: when someone enjoys a major unexpected "blessing," particularly financial, friends and kin may cajol them into sharing a part of it. What they share is called "balato."

balintawak: a close-fitting dress with butterfly sleeves, considered the national dress for women. Balintawak is also a place.

balut: a Filipino delicacy. A hard-boiled duck egg that has been incubated for a number of days.

bangka: canoe. There are many types, small and large, with one, two or no outriggers.

barkada: a tightly knit clique or peer group, usually of young people.

barong-barong: shanties.

barong tagalog: the formal Filipino shirt, usually embroidered, which evolved from the formal Spanish shirt. It is worn without a necktie, outside of the trousers, and is suitable for the most formal occasions.

barangay: meaning "boat," was traditionally a social unit like "a boatload," or the kinship group that came together in the boat. Now, a small political unit like a neighborhood.

barrio: a village, or a district of a municipality or a city.

bayan: can mean town, nation, a people.

bayanihan: traditional Filipino community action. This is especially common in the rural areas, and is typified by the moving of an entire house at once by friends and neighbors. The term "bayanihan" has come to be an important symbol of Filipinos' capacity to work together for a common goal.

BCCs: Base Christian Communities. Both a program and a phenomenon. Found largely, but not only in the rural areas, BCCs are small, local, democratically managed, usually Roman Catholic groups that engage in worship, study, reflection and action. Some have become highly political, believing that their faith calls them to help bring about major systemic change. Some, but not all of the Catholic bishops are sympathetic to BCCs.

belen: "Bethlehem," or nativity scene.

benevolent assimilation: a phrase commonly used to describe the McKinley Administration's Philippine policy during the early years of U.S. colonization.

bienvenida: a homecoming feast or party.

bundok: mountain. The American colloquialism "boondocks" comes from this word, and dates back to the Philippine-American war.

cabeza de barangay: the chief leader or administrator of a village.

calesa: a two-wheel, horse-drawn cart introduced by the Spaniards. It is usually for hire, and is still popular throughout the Philippines.

carabao: water buffalo (*Bubalus bubalis*), the main work animal of the Filipino peasant.

cock-fighting: a popular, highly institutionalized pastime. Both small, impromptu events and large, formal, public events are common, involving bouts between roosters especially bred to fight. It is usually accompanied by betting. The birds fight until one is totally defeated, usually dying.

colonial mentality: an attitude of dependence or inferiority (often accompanied by an undue respect toward those with lighter complexions) which in the Philippines has grown out of centuries of subservience to foreigners.

comity: a courtesy "understanding" or agreement. In the Philippines at the beginning of the American period, the major Protestant churches accepted what they called a "comity agreement," under which they agreed not to compete with one another, but to each work in certain specified areas. The comity agreement broke down after World War II.

common tao: "common person."

compadre (m), **comadre** (f): persons having a special relationship, usually created in connection with religious occasions such as baptisms or weddings. An example would be godparents. A way of extending one's "kinship system" through the

Spanish Catholic *compadrazco* system. The godfather is called "ninong," and the godmother is called "ninang" of the godchild. The godchild is called "inaanak," which literally means "created child," or the child/parent relationship resulting from the ritual.

conquistadores: the original armed Spanish conquerors.

convento: the priests' quarters.

datu: a tribal chieftain.

despedida: a farewell feast or party for someone who will be gone for a long time.

encomienda system: used during the Spanish times. Parts of the colony were apportioned to those who had helped in the conquest.

fiesta: a festival. At the community level, this is usually associated with the celebration of the life of a particular patron saint.

hacienda: an agricultural estate, usually large.

herbolario: a practitioner of traditional medicine, often using herbs.

hiya: sense of shame or deep embarrassment. Being placed in a socially unacceptable position.

hukbalahaps: the "Huks", or Hukbong Bayan Laban sa Hapon ("People's Liberation Army against Japan") operated mainly in Central Luzon during World War II, and then after the war sought to organize that area, with its long history of agrarian grievances, on a militant communist basis. By and large, this movement was subdued in the mid-1950s with much assistance from the U.S.

ilustrado: during the Spanish time, the children of the elite Filipinos who had been sent to Europe to study.

jeepney: a popular locally manufactured (and usually very colorfully decorated) public transport vehicle initially made from World War II Jeeps. Today many of them are extremely heavy duty, being made of light truck parts and having diesel engines, but with bodies that still resemble Jeeps.

kimona: a light upper garment for women, usually worn above a skirt such as a patadyong.

landlord: a land owner who has tenants.

lechon: a roast suckling pig, usually whole, cooked over a pit of coals from a wood fire, and usually prepared in connection with a popular set of recipes.

LIC: Low Intensity Conflict. A military doctrine aimed at counter-insurgency utilized by the U.S. in Central America and now in the Philippines, that is covered by operational manuals and other documents. It calls for highly secret operations, including the use of "dirty tricks," and seeks maximum impact in the political arena. It aims to avoid the use of American troops and encourages the use of "surrogates," including private persons and groups, to implement its "projects." It results in great confusion and suffering for ordinary people.

machismo: "male power," ultimately the power to dominate or destroy.

Malacanang Palace: the official residence of the president and his/her family.

mang: a term of respect similar to "mister," used with a proper name, as in "Mang Juan." Used mainly among ordinary folk.

mano po: a traditional respectful way for young people to greet older persons. The hand of the older person is taken by the younger and touched to his/her forehead, while saying "mano po".

merienda: a brief social time with a snack. A coffee or tea "break." A "merienda cena" is a heavier snack, usually served buffet style.

mestizo: one of mixed racial background. Now sometimes refers to someone having an unusually light complexion or Caucasian features.

Moro: a Muslim. The term was given by the Spanish, and for many years was considered derogatory. Now, however, Moro Filipinos claim the term with pride.

municipio: town.

ningas cogon: literally "grass fire," it refers to projects that start with great enthusiasm but then sputter and die out. Lack of staying power.

nipa: a low-growing palm that thrives in marshy areas and produces large quantities of tough leaves.

Popular for thatched roofs and for walls of village houses and shelters.

okay lang: a response to "how are you?" it is a sort of understatement for "I'm fine." Or, it can simply mean "okay."

oligarch: one of a powerful few.

pakikisama: smooth interpersonal relationships, ability to get along with others; camaraderie, togetherness; often requires yielding to group opinion.

palabas: a farcical show or program; sometimes used to refer to political events.

palay: unhusked grain, almost always of rice (in Tagalog and some other dialects); the rice plant growing in the field. In all dialects rice has specific words to describe its different forms and stages.

palengke: public market.

pancit: a popular noodle dish which is prepared in a variety of ways. (See Recipes in *The Sari-Sari Store: A Philippine Scrapbook.*)

parol: Christmas lantern. Usually in the shape of a five-pointed star, with streamers from the points.

pasalubong: gifts of travellers, food or other, brought back to friends and kin after even a short trip.

patadyong: a knee-length, close-fitting skirt.

peasants: generally means rural poor people who derive their subsistence livelihood from agriculture, as tenant farmers, as laborers, or working very small plots of their own.

pinoy: a Filipino (slang).

po: an interjection used when speaking to elders or superiors to show respect.

sala: the living room.

Santo Niño: image of the Holy Child.

sari-sari store: a tiny neighborhood variety store that sells personal and household items in small amounts, thi.1g. 'ike matches, cigarettes, cooking oil, kerosene, salt, pencils, notepaper, etc.

saya: a long skirt. "Under the saya" is a colloquial term for a henpecked husband!

sayang: "What a pity!"

sultan: a high chief of the Muslims.

tao: human being; person, humankind. "Common tao."

tinikling: an exciting popular folk dance using bamboo poles.

usury: lending at a rate of interest beyond that allowed by law.

utang na loob: debt of gratitude, or debt of the "inner self."

APPENDIX II

A Philippine Protestant Chronology

1898

August 28   The first Protestant services were held in the Philippines, conducted by Chaplain George Stull of the Methodist Episcopal Church, who had come with the American occupying forces. Attended by Filipinos as well as by military personnel.

1899

March 2   Bishop James M. Thoburn, missionary bishop for Southern Asia of the Methodist Episcopal Church, arrived to begin the first Protestant work in the Philippines. Presbyterian leader Dr. William H. Lingle had visited earlier, in December 1898, and his recommendation was that no mission be opened. His board had already taken action, however, and Dr. and Mrs. James Rodgers were already on their way to the Philippines when the report was received.

April   Dr. and Mrs. James Rodgers and Dr. and Mrs. David S. Hibbard of the Presbyterian Church arrived to become the first regularly appointed Protestant missionaries to the Philippines.

December   Dr. Rodgers organized the Philippine Presbyterian Mission.

     The Rev. and Mrs. Jay C. Goodrich opened the American Bible Society office in Manila.

1900

February   Three regularly appointed Methodist missionaries arrived: Dr. Annie Norton, Miss Julia Wisner and Miss Margaret Cody, all representing the Woman's Foreign Missionary Society. Miss Wisner organized the Manila Girls School, which was to become the Harris Deaconess school. Mrs. Cornelia Moots followed later the same year to work as a deaconess.

March   Nicolas Zamora, a disaffected Roman Catholic who had earlier become a Protestant, and whose father was the nephew of the nationalist priest Jacinto Zamora (hanged by the Spanish authorities), after being admitted on trial and elected to the order of deacon by the Southwest Kansas Annual Conference, was ordained by Methodist Bishop

Thoburn as the first Filipino Protestant preacher.

April   Dr. Eric Lund of the Baptist Mission arrived in Manila. After a few days he went on to Iloilo and Jaro to begin work in Capiz and the northern part of Panay.

July 6   General Arthur MacArthur issued a strongly written pledge to support strict separation of church and state and freedom of religion. This was endorsed by Protestant missionaries and generally supported by U.S. Catholics. It was denounced by Catholic authorities in the Philippines.

December   Miss Elizabeth White (who was to become Mrs. P.F. Jansen) arrived in Manila to begin the work of the Christian and Missionary Alliance. Their work was to center in Cotabato, Zamboanga and Jolo

1901

April   Edwin B. Eby and Sandford B. Kurtz arrived in Manila to begin the work of the United Brethren in Christ. They immediately moved their trunks and books to Vigan, and began their Ilocano language study. In 1903, The Rev. and Mrs. Howard W. Widdoes arrived, and were assigned to San Fernando, La Union. The work of the United Brethren was concentrated in the Vigan area, plus Baguio and the sub-provinces of Ifugao and Kalinga. The Ilocano Press at San Fernando was to publish many books and pamphlets, as well as several monthly papers.

April 24-26   The Evangelical Union of the Philippines was formed by representatives of the Presbyterian, Methodist Episcopal, and United Brethren Missions. The Baptist Mission joined soon afterward, and after a year the Congregational and Christian Missions joined. The purpose of the union was to further cooperation among the denominations at work in the Philippines. A notable accomplishment was the "Comity Agreement," which provided for territorial assignments for the participating churches.

August 28   The first classes were held in the school in Dumaguete, which was to become Silliman Institute and later, Silliman University. By 1904 there were already 90 students. In 1910 it offered a Bachelor of Arts degree, at that time the equivalent of 2 years' work.

October   The Methodist Publishing House was formally opened in Manila, called the Thoburn Press (finally sold in 1937).

Autumn   The Rev. and Mrs. W.H. Hanna and the Rev. Hermon P. Williams and family arrived in Manila to begin the work of the Disciples of Christ. That work was to include churches in and around Manila, Laoag, Ilocos Norte, Bangued and Abra.

The work of the Protestant Episcopal Church began with the arrival of the Revs. Walter Clapp and John A. Staunton and their wives. The Rev. Charles H. Brent, their first bishop, arrived about 6 months later. They devoted their efforts to work among the mountain people in Northern Luzon, in Southern Mindanao among the Tiruray, and among the Chinese in Manila.

1902

January

The Philippine Christian Advocate (produced by the Methodists) was begun, which by 1903 had 1000 subscribers.

The Presbyterian station was founded in Cebu by the Rev. and Mrs. P. Frederick Jansen.

The American Board Mission (Congregational) began its work with the arrival of Robert F. Black, who made his headquarters in Davao. This work included a hospital which was to become Broken-shire Hospital. A station was later opened (1914) at Cagayan, Misamis, with a hospital and training school for girls. A station in Lanao was also opened. The ABM actively participated in Silliman University as well.

1903

Harris Memorial School for girls was established by Miss Winnifred Spaulding, with 4 students. From 1905 until 1940 Harris, the training school for Methodist deaconesses, was under the leadership of Miss Marguerite Decker. In 1951, Prudencia L. Fabro became the first Filipina director. In 1988, the school, which has become Harris Memorial College, moved to a new campus at Taytay, Rizal.

1905

A Tagalog and an Ilocano hymnal were printed. Pampango and Pangasinan hymnals were begun. American Baptists established Jaro Industrial School (now Central Philippine University). The Christian and Missionary Alliance adopted the independent work of two missionary couples in Zamboanga. The Seventh-Day Adventists explored mission possibilities in the Philippines, prior to sending a missionary couple.

1906

The Ellinwood Bible Schools (Presbyterian), one for men and one for women, opened. This is now a part of Philippine Christian University.

Dr. Rebecca Parish founded Dispensaria Betania on the first floor of the Women's Bible School on Rizal Avenue. This was the "seed" that resulted in the Methodist Mary Johnston Hospital, as in 1908 Mr. D.S.B. Johnson gave money for the building of a hospital as a memorial to his wife, Mary. It was built at the edge of Manila Bay. In 1911, the Mary Johnston School of Nursing opened (now a part of Philippine Christian University).

The U.S. Supreme Court ruled that the Roman Catholic properties held by congregations of the Philippine Independent Church (see page 15) must be returned to the Catholic Church. This abruptly ended a period of extremely rapid growth of the Philippine Independent Church. At that time the PIC claimed 6 million members.

1907

Union Theological Seminary was begun by the Methodists and the Presbyterians, representing a union of the Florence B. Nicholson Seminary (organized in 1906 at Dagupan) and the Ellinwood Bible Training School (organized in 1905 in Manila). It was later to include the United Brethren (1911), the Disciples (1916) and the Congregationalists (1919). Instruction began in Spanish. By 1912, English had become the medium of instruction. The college department became known as Union College. A four-year high school was organized in 1919, an elementary school in 1947. The college eventually became Philippine Christian College, now Philippine Christian University.

1908

The founding of the University of the Philippines brought many students into Manila. This was to stimulate the founding of a number of church-related student dormitories.

The Philippine *Mission* Conference of the Methodist Church petitioned the General Conference against changing its status to that of *Annual* Conference, stating that this might be construed as inimical to the cause of Philippine independence. It did become an Annual Conference, however, and this was seen by nationalistic Filipinos as a sort of "annexation" to Methodism on the North American mainland.

May 1   Classes began at the Lingayen Bible Training School
                 for Women (Methodist).

1909

Feb. 28   Nicolas Zamora, a capable and nationalistic leader,
                 announced his withdrawal from the Methodist
                 Church and the formation of the IEMELIF (Iglesia
                 Evangelica Metodista en las Islas Filipinas). This was
                 done at St. Paul's Methodist Church in Tondo. Of
                 9 Filipino conference members, 4 followed Zamora,
                 as did 25 out of 121 local preachers. While the split
                 did involve issues related to nationalism, including
                 the powerful roles held by the missionary leaders,
                 it was precipitated by a bitter discussion related
                 to ministerial practices.

                 Seventh-Day Adventists begin work in the Philip-
                 pines through Mr. and Mrs. L.V. Finster.

1910

                 The San Fernando Bible Training School was
                 established in San Fernando, La Union.

1911

                 The Philippine Islands Sunday School Union was
                 organized, later renamed the Philippine Council of
                 Religious Education.

1912

                 Bishop William Eveland became the first resident
                 Methodist Bishop in the Philippines.

                 A Methodist dormitory was opened in Manila, later
                 to be known as Hugh Wilson Hall. Other dormitories
                 were to be opened in Vigan, San Fernando
                 Pampanga, Tarlac, Lingayen, Tuguegarao, Bayom-
                 bong, Cabanatuan and Manila. There were seven-
                 teen dormitories in operation by 1926, including
                 Rader Hall for men in Manila, the Presbyterian Girls'
                 Dorm, and the Disciples' Dorm for Girls.

1913

                 The Episcopal Church established Brent Hospital
                 in Zamboanga City.

1914

June 11   The Union Church of Manila was formally organized
                 by the American Presbyterian and Methodist
                 congregations.

                 The Methodist Philippines Annual Conference,

meeting in Vigan, passed a resolution requesting ministers of their church in the United States to refrain from speaking publicly either in favor of or against the independence of the Philippine Islands. At that conference, Marvin Rader, district superintendent of the Manila District, reported that the past year had been one of "extreme agitation" for independence from the United States.

Felix Manalo founded the Iglesia ni Kristo, which was to become a vigorous indigenous church.

1915

A plan was submitted by the Evangelical Union to form the Evangelical Christian Church of the Philippines, to be composed of all the newly established churches. This did not prove to be successful, but it paved the way for later efforts which would result in a National Christian Council.

1917

Presbyterian missionary Dr. Charles R. Hamilton established a residence at Los Baños to begin the work at the University of the Philippines center for agricultural training.

1918

The Jaro Industrial School was founded by the Baptists. This was to become a regular high school, then Central Philippines College, and later, Philippine Central University.

1919

The Methodist Church in the Philippines sent 5 teachers, graduates of the Normal School, to teach English in the Methodist School in Penang, Malaya.

1922

The Philippines Annual Conference of the Methodist Church passed a resolution putting itself on record "as being in entire sympathy with the national aspirations of the Filipino people... we declare our hearty approval of every constructive effort of the Filipinos looking towards the realization of these national aspirations." This was reaffirmed by the missionaries at the Annual Conference of 1926, and then in 1930 a similar resolution was sent to the United States Senate.

1924

The United Church of Manila was organized to

demonstrate the feasibility of church union.

D.D. Alejandro was elected the first non-missionary delegate to the Methodist General Conference.

1926

Union Theological Seminary moved to its Taft Avenue location, now the main campus of Philippine Christian University.

1928

The National Christian Council of the Philippines was formed, later to evolve into the Philippine Federation of Evangelical Churches, then the Philippine Federation of Christian Churches, and eventually the present National Council of Churches in the Philippines.

1929

The Presbyterian Church, the Evangelical United Brethren and the Congregational Churches united to form the United Evangelical Church of the Philippines, an autonomous evangelical church under national leadership. Enrique C. Sobrepena was elected Moderator.

1931

The UNIDA Church was founded, now a small but significant member communion of the NCCP.

1932

The first Filipino Methodist district superintendent was appointed.

1933

The second major split occurred in the Methodist Church, in San Nicolas, Pangasinan, led by the Rev. Cipriano Navarro and the Rev. Samuel Stagg, on the immediate basis of an ecclesiastical ruling, but also over the issue of self-determination by Filipinos in their religious affairs. 27 ordained ministers, 5 American missionaries and some deaconesses and Bible women left the conference, held a meeting of their own, and organized the Philippine Methodist Church. Its purpose was "preaching Methodism free from the control of the mother church" in the United States. In 1948 this church became one of the founding bodies of the United Church of Christ in the Philippines.

1936

The Methodist Philippines Annual Conference petitioned the General Conference for its own Central Conference and its own Filipino bishop. An enabling act was passed in 1940, and in 1944 Dr. D.D. Alejandro was elected the first Filipino bishop.

1938

The Philippine Federation of Evangelical Churches was organized by the United Evangelical Church, the Methodist Episcopal Church, the Baptist Convention, the Disciples, the IEMELIF and the UNIDA.

1940-41

War between Japan and China caused a great deal of dislocation among the missionaries of all denominations in the Far East, a number of whom went to the Philippines to serve.

1943

The Rev. Francisco Galvez was designated general superintendent of the Methodist Church in the Philippines, the first Filipino to be head of the church. This was during the Japanese occupation of World War II.

October   At the "request" of the Japanese, the Evangelical Church in the Philippines (the "Wartime Church") was founded by Iglesia Unida de Cristo, Iglesia Evangelica Christiano Independiente, the Church of Christ (Disciples), the Philippine Methodist Church (not to be confused with the Methodist Church in the Philippines, which did not join), part of the IEMELIF, and more than twenty smaller bodies. Enrique C. Sobrepena was elected presiding bishop.

1946

Philippine Wesleyan College was founded, now Wesleyan University - Philippines.

1948

The United Church of Christ in the Philippines was born as a merger of the United Evangelical Church of 1929, the Philippine Methodist Church and the Disciples of Christ. Cooperating with the UCCP at the present time, in addition to the American churches related to those original denominations, are the Reformed Church of America and the United Church of Canada.

Protestant work in the Philippines was significantly

affected by the transfer of missionaries from China who were unable to continue their work there. The Southern Baptists are an example. By 1951, more than 100 former American missionaries in China had been transferred to the Philippines.

1949

The first Methodist mobile clinic was deployed, assigned to the Cagayan Valley. It initially operated as the Church World Service Mobile Medical Clinic, supported by Church World Service funds. A mobile clinic was opened in Mindanao in 1954, and in the Northwest Philippines Annual Conference in 1955.

1950

A new hospital building was opened by Mary Johnston Hospital in Tondo.

The Methodist Social Center was founded in Sampaloc, Manila; it is now known as Kapatiran Kaunlaran.

1952

Dr. Benjamin I. Guansing was elected the first Filipino president of Union Theological Seminary.

The Methodist General Conference authorized the opening of Methodist work in Mindanao, where there were already twelve Methodist congregations in Cotabato alone, due to migration. In 1953, Esteban Guillermo and Calixto B. Garibay were sent as travelling elders to supervise the work, and in 1954 C. L. Spottswood and his wife Mariam were assigned as missionaries.

1961

A concordat was signed establishing full communion between the Philippine Independent Church and the Protestant Episcopal Church.

1962

Union Theological Seminary transferred to its present 97-hectare site at Dasmarinas Cavite.

1963

Formation of the National Council of Churches in the Philippines, successor to the Philippine Federation of Christian Churches (1949), the Philippine Federation of Evangelical Churches (1939), the National Christian Council (1929), the Evangelical Union (1901), and the Missionary Alliance (1900).

1965

The Philippine Council of Evangelical Churches was organized. Charter member groups included the Conservative Baptist Association of the Philippines; Christian and Missionary Alliance; International Foursquare Gospel Church; Inter-Varsity Christian Fellowship; New Tribes Mission; and a number of nondenominational congregations sponsored by such service organizations as Far Eastern Gospel Crusade, Far East Broadcasting Company, Overseas Missionary Fellowship, Philippine Missionary Fellowship, and Fellowship of Indigenous Fundamental Churches of the Philippines.

1972

September 21   Martial law was declared, which had great impact upon a number of important ministries of the churches, and which proved to be an extremely divisive issue.

1974

Amendments to the Laurel-Langley agreement meant that Americans could not own property in the Philippines. It was required that all real estate owned by American mission agencies be turned over to Philippine institutions.

1986

February 22   The four-day "People's Power Revolution" began, with the active participation of many churchpeople.

Prepared by B. David Williams with the assistance of Byron W. Clark and T. Valentino Sitoy, Jr.

BIBLIOGRAPHY

Alejandro, Dionisio D. *From Darkness to Light,* Manila: Board of Communications and Publications, Philippines Central Conference of the United Methodist Church, 1974.

Anderson, Gerald H. *Studies in Philippine Church History,* Ithaca and London: Cornell University Press, 1969.

Brown, Arthur Judson. *The New Era in the Philippines,* New York: Fleming H. Revell Co., 1903.

Clymer, Kenton J. *Protestant Missionaries in the Philippines, 1898-1916.* Urbana and Chicago: University of Illinois Press, 1986.

Deats, Richard. *Nationalism and Christianity in the Philippines,* Dallas: Southern Methodist University Press, 1967.

Deats, Richard. *The Story of Methodism in the Philippines*, Manila: Rangel & Sons, 1964.

Higdon, Dr. and Mrs E.K. *From Carabao to Clipper*, New York: Friendship Press, 1941 (Disciples of Christ).

Laubach, Frank C. *The People of the Philippine Islands*, New York, George H. Doran Co., 1925.

McLeish, Alexander. *A Christian Archipelago*, London: World Dominion Press, 1941.

Roberts, Walter N. *The Filipino Church*, Dayton, Ohio: Foreign Missionary Society, United Brethren in Christ, 1936 (mainly about the work of the United Brethren in Christ).

Rodgers, James B. *Forty Years in the Philippines* (A History of the Philippine Mission of the Presbyterian Church in the United States of America, 1899-1939). New York: The Board of Foreign Missions of the Presbyterian Church in the U.S.A., 1940.

Sobrepena, Enrique C. *That They May Be One,* 2nd ed., Manila: United Church of Christ in the Philippines, 1964 (brief account of the movement that let to the formation of the UCCP).

Spottswood, Curran L. *Beyond Cotabato*, Westwood, New Jersey: Fleming H. Revell Co., 1961 (Methodist work in Mindanao after 1954).

Stuntz, Homer C. *The Philippines and the Far East*, Cincinnati: Jennings and Pye, 1904 (Protestant beginnings).

APPENDIX III

An Outline of Christian Churches in the Philippines

Approximately 85 percent of the people in the Philippines identify themselves as Roman Catholic.

There is a greater variety and number of separate Christian groups in the Philippines than in any country in Asia, with the possible exception of Japan.

The Philippines is among the top three recipients of U.S.-based Christian mission agencies in the world: There are 150 such agencies in the Philippines (pop. 57 million), as compared with 161 in Mexico (pop. 80 million), and 155 in India (pop. 800 million). This is without counting the direct sending of missionaries by local congregations in the U.S., sometimes called the "faith missionaries," who work independently and whose support is sometimes uncertain.

The Roman Catholic Church:

There are 71 ecclesiastical territories (16 archdioceses, 49 dioceses, 5 prelatures, and 1 military ordinary), with 2 cardinals, 14 archbishops, and 78 bishops. 1987 sources report a total of 2,144 parishes with approximately 45,906,000 members, of a total population of 54,380,000 (84.4 percent). Assuming a present Philippine population of approximately 57 million, the Roman Catholic Church probably has a total constituency of more than 48 million.

Member bodies of the National Council of Churches in the Philippines:

Christ-Centered Church
Convention of Philippine Baptist Churches
Iglesia Evangelica Metodista en las Islas Filipinas
Iglesia Evangelica Unida de Cristo
Iglesia Filipina Independiente
Lutheran Church in the Philippines
Philippine Episcopal Church
Salvation Army
United Church of Christ in the Philippines
United Methodist Church

(The NCCP has a combined constituency of over 5 million members.)

NCCP Associate Members:

Association of Christian Schools and Colleges (over 70 member schools)
Consortium of Christian Organizations in Rurban (Rural-Urban) Development
The Holt International Children's Services
Manila Community Services, Inc.
The Philippine Bible Society (approximately 35 Protestant denominations and Christian organizations, in cooperation with the Roman Catholic Church
Student Christian Movement of the Philippines
Union Church of Manila (an international congregation)

Member bodies of the Philippine Council of Evangelical Churches (26 denominations):

Association of Bible Churches of the Philippines, Inc. (ABCOP)
Baptist Conference of the Philippines, Inc. (BCP)
Calvary Gospel Tabernacle, Inc.
Charismatic Full Gospel Ministries, Inc.
Christ Faith Fellowship OHM Philippines, Inc.
Christ to the Philippines, Inc.
Christian Catholic Church (Evangelical) of the Philippines, Inc.
Christian Evangelical Missions, Inc.
Christian & Missionary Alliance Churches of the Philippines, Inc. (CAMACOP)
Church of God World Missions of the Philippines, Inc.
Church of the Foursquare Gospel of the Philippines, Inc.
Church of the Nazarene, Philippines, Inc.
Conservative Baptist Association of the Philippines, Inc.
Evangelical Free Church of the Philippines, Inc.
First Pentecostal Church of God of the Philippines, Inc.
General Baptist Churches of the Philippines, Inc.
Grace Evangelical Mission, Inc.
Independent Baptist Churches in the Philippines, Inc.
Kalahan Cooperative Parish
Northern Mindanao Advent Christian Conference, Inc.

Philippine General Council of the Assemblies of God, Inc.
Philippine Missionary Fellowship, Inc.
The Philippine Conference of Free Methodist Church, Inc.
The Salvation Army, Philippine Territory, Inc.
The Wesleyan Church, Inc.
World Missionary Evangelism, Inc.

Various local churches

46 Associate Members such as:

Christian Literature Crusade, Inc.
Inter-varsity Christian Fellowship, Inc.
Overseas Missionary Fellowship, Inc.
Far Eastern Gospel Crusade
The Navigator Ministries, Inc.

various seminaries and Bible schools, missions, broadcasting networks, evangelism crusades

Member bodies of the Division of Overseas Ministries of the National Council of the Churches of Christ in the U.S.A. (DOM) having work in the Philippines:

American Baptist Churches International Ministries
Christian Church (Disciples of Christ)
Church of God, Anderson, Indiana (affiliate)
Episcopal Church, World Mission
General Conference, Seventh Day Adventist (affiliate)
Mennonite Central Committee (fraternal)
Presbyterian Church (U.S.A.)
Reformed Church in America World Ministries
United Board for Christian Education in Asia
United Church Board for World Ministries
United Methodist Board of Global Ministries, World Program Division

37 members of the Evangelical Foreign Missions Association (EFMA) have work in the Philippines, including:

Assemblies of God Foreign Missions, Baptist General Conference Missions, Campus Crusade for Christ Intl., Christian Missionary Alliance, Foursquare Missions International.

11 members of the Interdenominational Foreign Mission Association of North America, Inc. (IFMA) **have work in the Philippines, including:**

> Back to the Bible Missionary Agency, Overseas Missionary Fellowship USA

2 members of the Associated Missions of the International Council of Christian Churches (TAM-ICCC) have work in the Philippines

2 members of the Fellowship of Missions (FOM) have work in the Philippines

Others that maintain a high degree of separateness:

> Church of Christ, Scientist
> Christian Missions in Many Lands
> Church of Jesus Christ of the Latter Day Saints
> Jehovah's Witnesses
> Southern Baptist Convention
> Wycliff Bible Translators

Indigenous movements:

> Iglesia ni Kristo
> Indigenous churches resulting from schism
> The Rizalist movement: many groups, some with and some without a degree of Christian identity
> "Nativistic movements" rooted in traditional religion and culture, but using Christian concepts in an attempt to revitalize the tradition. Some rather esoteric.
> The Espiritista Movement (Union Espiritista Cristiana de Filipinas)
> Groups first officially organized among Filipino emigrants in California and Hawaii and later brought to the Philippines, such as World Peace Crusaders Mission (The Lamplighters)

SOURCES:

Catholic Almanac, 1988, produced by *Our Sunday Visitor*, for which the source was *Honorario Pontificio*, 1987.

Elwood, Douglas. "Varieties of Christianity in the Philippines", a chapter in Anderson, Gerald, *Studies in Philippine Church History*, Ithaca and London: Cornell U. Press, 1969.

Missions Advanced Research and Communications Center (MARC), *Mission Handbook*, 13th ed., Monrovia, CA: MARC, 1986.

Philippine Council of Evangelical Churches, roster of member bodies.

APPENDIX IV

Filipinos in the United States

Tens of thousands of Filipinos have left their own land seeking better economic opportunity. Approximately 2.5 million Filipinos have gone out to over 117 countries, truly a community "in dispersion!" The major concentrations of Filipinos are as follows:[*]

Australia	25,000
Canada	100,000
Japan	10,916 (excluding illegal entrants)
Hong Kong	36,000
Singapore	28,000
Malaysia	100,000
Middle East	600,000 (300,000 in Saudi Arabia)
Italy	80,000
West Germany	16,000 (registered)
France	7,000
United Kingdom	25,000 to 30,000
Spain	50,000
United States	1.5 million (approx. 500,000 are illegal)

Each of these communities has its own character. In Hong Kong it is mostly female, mostly domestic helpers; in Japan, predominantly "entertainers" and seamen; in the Middle East (about 80 percent in Saudi Arabia), largely male technicians, drivers and laborers; in Brunei, Guam, Papua New Guinea, Fiji, Palau and other Pacific islands are found groups of a few hundred Filipino construction workers and professionals and their families.

Muslim refugees and settlers make up one of the larger Filipino expatriate groups, mostly in Sabah, Malaysia, working in plantation and logging areas.

Approximately 75 percent of the overseas Filipinos are under 40 years of age and therefore in their most productive years. As a group they send large amounts of money back to the Philippines (a very conservative estimate puts the amount at about U.S. $3.4 billion for the period between

---

[*] Sources: *Philippines Migration Review.* Vol II, No. 2, 1987, and figures made available by the Asia-Pacific Mission for Migrant Filipinos, 4 Jordan Rd., Kowloon, Hong Kong.

1978 and 1983). In 1987, 496,854 Filipino overseas contract workers remitted U.S. $791.91 million.

Between 1965 and 1974, the U.S. was the destination of 82.5 percent of all Filipinos leaving their country. According to an unofficial estimate by the Philippine Embassy in Washington, D.C., there are currently around 1.5 million Filipinos in the U.S., including Filipino-Americans (U.S. citizens) as well as Philippine citizens. This is the largest settled Filipino community outside the Philippines.

According to the 1980 census, there were 774,652 Filipinos in the U.S., more than twice the number of those present in 1970 (336,371). More than half were living in California (45.8 percent) and Hawaii (16.9 percent). They lived predominantly in urban areas (92.4 percent).

While the earlier immigrants were mostly men, the male/female ratio is about even today (51.7 percent male). The women have a higher educational attainment than men (14.4 vs. 13.5 median school years completed). The women receive incomes, however, that are almost half those of men, a situation that prevails with women of all ethnic/racial groups.

A relatively high number of Filipinos (25.1 percent) are employed in the higher-level occupations, and a relatively high number are either underemployed or overeducated for the jobs they hold.

The Philippines has exported more nurses than any other country in the world, and more doctors than any other country except India. A substantial number of these are in the United States. Other groups of higher-level professional Filipinos are also found in the U.S., even a growing number of Filipino clergy.

In 1980, Filipinos were the second largest ethnic minority from Asia, after the Chinese. Filipinos were also outnumbered by blacks, Hispanics and Native Americans.

It is not well known that some Filipinos lived in America long before the Spanish-American War. As early as the mid-1700s, a "Manila Village" existed in Jefferson Parish, Louisiana, composed mainly of Filipino seamen. This was even before Louisiana was part of the U.S.!

Americans do not sufficiently appreciate what heartache the early Filipino immigrants experienced, nor what an important contribution, past and present, Filipino immigrants have made to American life and well-being. Filipino medical professionals are a case in point, with their caring, enthusiasm and eagerness to participate.

Not until the beginning of this century, and more particularly in the 1920s, was the movement of Filipinos carefully documented. Recruiting of Filipino labor for Hawaii (and some for the mainland) started as early as 1905. It increased with an experimental group of 150 in 1907, and then accelerated with the passage of the Immigration Acts of 1920 and 1924, which barred the immigration of Japanese. Between 1907 and 1930 an estimated 150,000 Filipinos came to the U.S., more than half of them to Hawaii.

Filipino students coming to the U.S. before 1920 were readily accepted because of their sponsorship by missionary-related educational institutions and the U.S. government; they were predominantly from the middle and upper socio-economic classes.

Unlike other non-white foreigners coming to the U.S., Filipinos, because of the status of their country as a U.S. colony, were not considered aliens, but "nationals." Thus they could not be deported. Neither could they vote, however, and it was difficult for them to become citizens. Anti-Asian laws were used to prevent them from owning property, and anti-miscegenation laws (prohibiting mixing of the races) were specifically directed at them, even well into the post World War II period.[*]

When Commonwealth status was declared in 1935, Filipino immigration was limited to 50 persons per year, and the Welch Bill (H.R. 6464) appropriated $300,000 to pay the fare of Filipinos who would voluntarily return to the Philippines. The powerful Hawaiian Sugar Planters Association, however, was able to continue bringing in laborers in relatively large numbers even after 1934.

The story of Filipinos in the U.S. Navy is fascinating in itself,[†] and as early as 1919 there were as many as 6,000. Between 1944 and 1973, at least 22,000 were recruited into the U.S. Navy. The several generations of those who participated claim a common experience: until recently, they were required to serve as stewards, serving officers by cleaning their living quarters, caring for their uniforms, serving their meals and washing their dishes (and, not

---

[*] Anti-miscegenation laws were declared unconstitutional in California in 1948, but were retained by some states as late as 1967.

[†] For greater detail on this story, see Jesse G. Quinsaat, "How to Join the Navy and Still Not See the World," *Letters in Exile, An Introductory Reader on the History of Pilipinos in America* (Los Angeles: UCLA Asian American Studies Center, 1976).

uncommonly, asked to do personal "outside" chores for officers and their wives).

In 1973, 9,000 of the 11,000 stewards in the U.S. Navy were Filipinos. Interestingly, Filipinos were allowed to join the U.S. Navy as foreign nationals because of the Military Bases Agreement, signed by the U.S. and the Philippines in 1947, and nowhere in the agreement does it state that Filipinos were expressly recruited to be stewards. Despite this history of Filipinos becoming stewards, there has been no lack of applicants, largely due to the severe economic conditions prevailing in the Philippines.

Over the years and until now, most Filipino immigrants to the U.S. have had to face racism in one form or another. The earlier immigrants were at a special disadvantage in coping with racism at a time when it was severe and overt. The poignant stories of Carlos Bulosan[*] give a touching, disturbing insight into the plight of Filipino workers in American prior to World War II. In the words of labor advocate and writer Carey McWilliams, Bulosan gave us "a clearer view of society by being on the bottom looking up."

From 1935 to 1964 the immigration of Filipinos into the U.S. was greatly limited by racially based quotas. The U.S. Immigration and Nationality Act of 1965 resulted in a much larger number of Filipino immigrants, and due to its provisions, those allowed to come were of a much higher educational standing and socio-economic status. The loss of these professional Filipinos is what many in the Philippines would later call their "brain drain."

Research indicates that conditions in the Philippines, more than perceptions of life outside, were the major factor for emigrating. It was more "push" than "pull." Since Spanish times the national economy has been basically export-oriented, and local business and professional opportunities have been seriously limited (from the standpoint of economic attractiveness). Major agricultural innovations, which were generally for the sake of export activity, were of decreasing labor intensity. Over the years most ordinary Filipino producers were discouraged and limited by market forces and by maldistribution of land from producing more than what subsistence required.

---

[*] See Bulosan, *America Is In the Heart* (Seattle and London: University of Washington Press, 1973, first published in 1943 by Harcourt, Brace and Co., Inc.). Bulosan's poem, "'ette' 'n Fxile" appears on page 181.

As the Philippines became somewhat "Americanized," the use of English became very common and American success models and images became the ideal for many, even in the Philippine context. Yet those models became increasingly difficult to realize. Many Filipinos sought to go elsewhere to pursue those aspirations.

Population pressure in itself has contributed significantly to the "push," as the Philippines' population has been doubling approximately every 20 years.

A critical (but not uncommon) view holds that the exodus of large numbers of Filipinos for the United States and other places has relieved some of the pressures in the Philippines for desperately needed political and economic change, and that the receiving economies, particularly that of the U.S., have been provided with categories of labor and professional skill that they neither wanted to nor could provide for themselves. Certainly the Philippines has lost some of its most talented people, with Americans among the greatest beneficiaries.

The continued attention being given by Filipinos to the story of Filipino immigrants to America seems to indicate that unresolved issues remain.

B.D.W.

REFERENCES:

Asia-Pacific Mission for Migrant Filipinos (APMMF). *Proceedings of the First Regional Consultation of Migrant Filipinos*, Dec. 5-7, 1985. Hong Kong, APMMF, 1986; and correspondence providing more recent statistics.

McWilliams, Carey. Introduction to Bulosan, Carlos. *America is In the Heart*. Seattle and London: University of Washington Press, 1973.

Philippine Resource Center (PRC). *In the Belly of the Beast: The Filipino Community in the U.S.* Berkeley: PRC, 1985.

Pido, J.A., Antonio. *The Pilipinos in America*. New York: Center for Migration Studies, 1985.

Quinsaat, Jesse, Ed. *Letters in Exile, An Introductory Reader on the History of Pilipinos in America*. Los Angeles: UCLA Asian American Studies Center, 1976.

U.S. Bureau of the Census. *Census of Population: 1980*. Characteristics of the Population, Vol. 1, Chapter C. PC80-1. General Social and Economic Characteristics, U.S. Summary. December 1983.

Letter in Exile
by Carlos Bulosan

Hourly the planes scour the skies to chart
The uncharted defenses of their loved country.
It is summer and the waiting steamers will
Unload by the sounding sea, to fill the needs
Of cities falling in the hunger of working man;
While the green hills widen their luxuriant
Shoulders of sharp glades, caught in the palm
Of the determinate sun, born of the islands.

All seems to concentrate on their way.
They make millions and their sons enter night clubs.
Bright virgin girls moan and bleed in their beds.
They close banks and their daughters throw money
To titled foreign gentlemen and cynical waiters.
Their bourgeois homes are wrecked. Into the streets
They pursue the course of their passion. They hold
Life in bubbles of drunkenness and fancy.

Knowing the tremendous web of this mistake,
I think of our favorite little islands
Cupped in those dovelike moving seas,
And our paternal homestead where exuberant
Brothers and silent sisters met every morning
To exhibit all ways of courtesy.
We were passionate in those days. Our parents
Condoned no dishonesties and personal indecencies.

Recalling all this before the hour of midnight,
I remembered you, brother, and hoped you
Could watch with me the splendid glide
of limousines in this street, and in that other,
The long parade of hungry working men
That approached my window at dawn to remind
Me once again of the coughing orbit of life
In this strange land, their loved country.

We didn't have the poet's vision of the hangman's
Dream to twist the whole of living on our finger,
But in those islands, under familiar trees we spoke
Of the littlest things with the simplest joys.

There were no books and hard intellectual thoughts,
But we grew into manhood with the music of trees
In our hearts that would not break, breaking
At last to the barrenness of hard city streets.

All of it was anxiety. All the years that passed.
And I am still facing a greater anxiety;
The promised happiness that never came to me.
Ten years for me and twelve for you, and that other,
The other younger brother who could not find himself,
Fifteen years—and he was only a child when he came.
But we are still here burning with a thousand fevers,
Though now more discerning, the enemy close at hand.

I was God's wonder boy: but if I did not
Defile the greed of mad men, if I did not save
Beauty from the naked blasphemies of money,
You must know that I cried when the Jews
Were driven from their country, when the Negroes
Were burned in their homes. You must know
That with these feeble hands I crept to the window
Unashamed to die in a world gone mad with power.

Power and greed will ravage beauty and give us
Loneliness. But all this will come to pass.
So live the New Year flooding the city with noises,
Like the tragic noises of revolution, that reach me
Like a heartstroke. And all will move forward
On the indiscriminate course of history that never
Stops to rectify our tragic misgivings and shame.

From *Letters in Exile,* edited by Dolores S. Feria, Quezon City, 1960 as printed in Quinsaat, ed. *Letters in Exile, op. cit.*

APPENDIX V

This resolution was forwarded to the general secretary of the National Council of the Churches of Christ in the USA, urging a positive response in support of the removal of the bases from the Philippines.

RESOLUTION
On Peace and the U.S. Military Bases in the Philippines

WHEREAS, the past NCCP, Conventions have taken a position opposing the continued presence of U.S. military bases in the Philippines as a threat to peace and/or sovereignty as a people;

WHEREAS, the NCCP, in line with Christian principles, still stands for the cause of peace and still opposes threats to lasting peace;

WHEREAS, THE NCCP, in fostering stronger ecumenical relationships with other Christian bodies in all lands, enjoin other Christians in common pursuit of peace;

NOW, THEREFORE RESOLVED AS IT IS HEREBY RESOLVED,

1) That the NCCP hold a National Consultation on the U.S. Military Bases in the Philippines to better inform the member churches about this issue;

2) That the NCCP, in recognition of the upcoming U.S. National Ecumenical Study Theme sponsored by the NCCC/USA, urge the NCCC/USA and its member-communions to study the effects of the U.S. military bases in the Philippines and to consider joining the NCCP in its long-standing opposition to the continued presence of these bases and facilities as a threat to peace and security not only to the Filipino people but also to the people of the Asia/Pacific region.

The General Convention
The National Council of Churches in the
    Philippines
November 27, 1987